T0247386

I Kissed a Ghost
a Ghost
(and I Liked It)

I Kissed a Ghost

a Ghost

(and I Liked It)

A Jersey Girl's Reality Show... with Dead People

Concetta Bertoldi

Mango Publishing
CORAL GABLES

Cover Design: Linda Echebevrry ART DESIGN
Cover Photo: Jim Beckner
Layout & Design: Liz Hong

For permission requests, please contact the publisher at:
Mango Publishing Group
2850 S Douglas Road, 2nd Floor
Coral Gables, FL 33134 USA
info@mango.bz

For special orders, quantity sales, course adoptions and corporate sales, please email the publisher at sales@mango.bz. For trade and wholesale sales, please contact Ingram Publisher Services at customer.service@ingramcontent.com or +1.800.509.4887.

I Kissed a Ghost and I Liked It: A Jersey Girl's Reality Show...with Dead People

Library of Congress Cataloging-in-Publication number: 2019938549
ISBN: (print) 978-1-64250-041-7, (ebook) 978-1-64250-042-4
BISAC category code: OCC022000, BODY, MIND & SPIRIT / Afterlife & Reincarnation

Printed in the United States of America

This book is dedicated to my husband, John Bertoldi, a truly wonderful man, husband, father, and friend! I have watched John for over thirty-five years with amazement. John has great integrity, loyalty, and heart. He has taught me the importance of patience. He has given all he has to give to his children and those he loves, never finding it necessary to mention it once he has given it! It's fair to say John is the only man I've ever dated with enough self-confidence to never be jealous of my outgoing personality! In short, John knows who he is and enjoys himself, and he has allowed me the space and freedom to be *myself*. He has happily supported my work right from the beginning. Marriage is a special bond made of trust, respect, love, and commitment. John has shown me all of that, and much more! He remembers that romance is not only for newlyweds and lovers alone. We have always had a common destiny. Simply, home is not home without my husband John in it. He is the best thing life has brought me. John, I love you always.

Table of Contents

Introduction

There's No Business like Show Business

When I was five years old, my mother enrolled me in a children's tap-dance group that met every Saturday morning. As a wrap-up to the season, my group of about fifteen girls was to put on a little recital for our parents, singing "How Much Is that Doggie in the Window?" On the day of our performance, my mother was in the hospital—she had just given birth to my younger brother Bobby—so my aunt and uncle came to my show in her place. I was very excited to perform the song and dance for a room packed with parents, but, when it was time to go on, I suddenly didn't want to dance and sing with the other girls. I wanted the stage all to myself. I'm not sure what compelled me; all I know is that I didn't go on with them. I waited in the wings until they had completed their little routine. I watched them all tap-dance off, and then I stepped up to center stage to give the room my solo performance, doing the whole song and dance again, on my own—to much laughter and applause, I might add! The audience went nuts, and I got my first standing ovation.

When my aunt went to visit my mother later that day, my mother was holding brand-new-baby Bobby in her arms, but instead of saying, "Oh, what a beautiful baby!" the first words out of her mouth were, "Oh my God, Eleanor! You will never guess what Concetta did!"

My whole life, I had always been comfortable in front of people. I loved the feeling of having a microphone in my hand and being on the stage. As a kid, I used to think I would be an actress. (I know I've had another life when I was an actress, but I'll say more about that later.) I never would have imagined that what would bring me to the stage this time around would be helping to deliver messages from the other side as a psychic medium. I have been hearing dead people all my life, and, from the time I was a kid, I would bring messages to my neighbors from their deceased

loved ones. Since going public with my ability, I have been doing
the same for thousands of clients, every day, in my office in New
Jersey. I go on stage regularly now. And it is a performance. But
it's also authentic. I try to cheer up my guests and bring them
comfort, so I'll crack a joke from time to time, but the messages
are real and are validated over and over, in each and every show.
I never take credit for the messages—the helpful spirits over
there are telling me everything, sometimes even pretty crazy
stuff that I don't understand myself—so when the messages are
validated, their loved ones can know for sure that it's really the
spirits, that "dead" is not dead. They are still here among us,
all the time.

If you're holding this book, chances are someone you love on
the other side led you to it. That's one of the things our deceased
loved ones do for us. They *guide* us to make choices that help
keep us on our divine path. Of course, here on the earth plane,
we still have free will, and we often make a wrong turn, but our
dead folks on the other side are constantly trying to re-route our
GPS and get us back on track.

That's a lot of what I want to talk about in this book. In my last
book, I discussed "soul contracts" and the agreements we make
before coming here—generally agreeing to taking on certain
challenges, or maybe working within certain limitations, in
order to learn a particular life lesson or deal with some karma
accumulated in other lives. Basically, we take on a new role
each time; we interact with other characters, try different
relationships or occupations, and deal with the challenges each
new situation brings. When Shakespeare said, "All the world's
a stage, and all the men and women merely players," he wasn't
kidding. But the earth plane is less like a play with every line

scripted than it is like a reality show—there's an outline based on the agreements we've made, but anything can happen!

I believe each of us chooses our role with a *divine purpose* before coming here to earth. Certain aspects of what we might think of as our personality are core parts of who we are. Just like an actor playing multiple roles, aspects of ourselves are recognizable in each lifetime. I know I've chosen to be on the stage in many lifetimes because it feels so familiar. Originally, I thought my divine purpose was to sing show tunes because I so loved being and singing in front of people. I found out later that, while I *have* had a lifetime as an actress, in *this* lifetime I would be using my comfort on the stage to heal and connect people to their loved ones on the other side.

In this reality show on earth, we may audition many times before landing our role. Are we a New Jersey Housewife? Are we an Undercover Boss? An Iron Chef or a Top Model? Are we a Survivor? We speak our lines, form showmances, strategize, and use our practiced skills; it often can feel like a competition, although, in this reality show, that's certainly not the overall point. We interact with various other cast members (teachers, coworkers, neighbors, friends, salespeople, and service providers), we put on holiday dinners, go to work, and take the kids to school. But here, instead of cameras following our every move, we have the spirits of our deceased loved ones watching over our shoulders. They act more like producers, but ones who want you personally to win! They send signs and signals all the time, and can sometimes arrange "chance meetings," introducing an important new character to your show. The help they give us is critical to our success and well-being.

Human life is about struggling, experiencing, and learning. There are skinned knees, broken friendships, lost jobs, and terrible things like war, poverty, abuse, and addictions. There is a whole lot of joy, and even miracles, but I don't think anyone gets all the good stuff without some of the other. Life on earth is just crazy hard. I see clients all day long who are carrying guilt and shame and fear. They are being held back from the joy and perfection available to them, and I can relate to their stories in so many ways. Your loved ones on the other side know of your struggles and they want to help. They want to remind you of your divine purpose and why you came here to be the star of your own reality show.

In this book, I hope to share some wisdom for the living, as well as some exceptional insights from the dead. In a way, the dead have it easy—they've crossed over into the "unconditional love" zone of the spiritual plane. Here on the material plane, we are still dealing with unresolved guilt and shame, regrets, family drama, and arguments over who's going to get Grandma's wedding ring. It's hard work being on earth. And not even a psychic medium has it all figured out.

As you read, you'll notice I'm a big fan of God, and I will talk about God in these pages. In my world, he carries the big guns. I often say, "In the name of God, hear my prayer." It makes me feel strong and supported. That said, I was raised to love all religions, and don't favor any one religion over another. (Although I love giving Christmas gifts, I gotta admit!) So, when that word "God" comes up, you can take it and swap it out for whatever makes you feel comfortable.

I hope in these pages you will find comfort for any sorrows you may have, and feel uplifted by the knowledge that those you have loved will never leave you. I hope you may find some ideas here that will support your journey in this crazy reality show here on earth.

With love,

Concetta Bertoldi

Chapter 1

Nobody's Perfect: A Bit about Me

I don't remember a time when I didn't hear the dead—that is to say, the spirits of the deceased, who are always here around us. When I was a kid in the 1950s, my mother used to freak out because she would frequently see me talking to people who weren't there. To me it was normal, and fortunately the idea that there are some of us who have this ability is becoming more accepted. If this were the 1700s, I'd be in the town square and there'd be a fire going!

My relationship with the spirits has changed over the years—in a sense, my experience of how I hear them has matured. Like most people, I don't remember a lot of details from my earliest experiences when I was very young. My parents certainly noticed and told me later what they had observed. Apparently, I was quite matter-of-fact about hearing the other side.

I remember my father constantly schooling me on how to handle this. His own father, my grandfather, had been an incredible medium, so my abilities were somewhat old hat to him, nothing shocking. I remember him saying, "Remember that your mind is not like other people's. Your mind is different. Your mind is stronger than other people's."

I didn't completely understand what he meant, but in my soul I understood. I never thought to say to him, "Well, can you explain to me how this is?" I was about ten at the time, and what does a ten-year-old know? Other than to say, "Okay, Daddy," and just know that he loves me, and I trust him, and so it must be true. Something inside me told me that yes, it was true, and that I would find out more as I got older. I remember being very much aware of the other side and being under its protection. I remember feeling that I was being guarded.

What most stands out for me at the beginning is that I often had what some would call an intuitive sense about people, knowing who could be trusted and who couldn't. Sometimes it would be a place that I either knew intuitively was either okay or off-limits, rather than a specific person, but I definitely had strong feelings about where I was and who I was with.

When I was twelve or thirteen, I did a lot of babysitting, making a whopping fifty cents an hour. I had one job working for a woman I will call "Joan." Her husband was never home, so, when she had to go out, I would watch her two children, one about nine months and the other maybe two years old. I felt such sadness around this lady, but never felt threatened by her. One night when I was at her house, the kids long in bed, her husband came in. He was a cop, so you would think I would be safe. Think again.

As soon as he came in and said, "Hello," I immediately felt *danger*. Bad energy!

All my life, I've had constant guardian angels. Most of the time, these were spirits whom I'd never known on earth. On this particular night, a female energy spirit, who I think may have been my grandmother who I'd never met (my mother's mother died very young, at the age of twenty-seven), was looking out for me.

I was a young kid with hair in curlers, just wanting to be paid the $2.50 I'd earned. But I heard my guardian angel say: *"Leave right away!"*

"What do we owe you?" he asked.

I was making my way to the door as I said, "Two dollars and fifty cents."

He said, "What's your hurry? Why don't you sit down on the couch? Let's talk."

I heard, very loud: *"Leave now!"*

I told him, no, I'd collect my money the next day from Joan. And then I *ran* home. I later heard that they had divorced and she moved away. I hope she found happiness.

***

Many times in my life, I have been warned by spirits. As a teenager, I didn't want to be bothered with a bunch of dead people, as I thought of them then, on the other side. I really just wanted to be a teenager and enjoy all that that entailed. But they were always there.

When I was fifteen, I was still pretty immature and innocent. I went to school with a girl I'll call "Mary" whose brother was dating another girl a little older than us—the two were always together. At that age, when you're seeing a teenage couple, you can't help being a little envious and wondering what it would be like if you, too, had a boyfriend. But teenage love is rarely perfect and in this case it was tragic. One day at school, I heard the news that Mary's brother had shot himself over his girlfriend. Her sadness and pain were obvious—I felt so sorry for her. I remember being in class and seeing her sitting at her desk and her brother right next to her, in spirit form. I wanted so much to tell her but just couldn't. I was a young teenager, trying to fit in. And this was the 1960s—well before anyone really talked about psychic abilities. And how can you explain what you don't even understand yourself? All I wanted was to be "normal," whatever that meant. I just wanted the spirits to leave me alone. Now that my own brother has crossed, I understand even more deeply the pain she was feeling. I wish so much that I could go back and hug her and tell her that her brother is with God, loved and safe.

When I was nineteen, I fell in love. I mean really in love, the kind of love you feel only once. I'll call him "Sam" to protect the innocent. Sam was so hot, I felt like ice cream left out in the sun. I was just *hungry* for him, and I still think of him fondly, the memories stirring mind, body, and soul. Anyone who has read my previous books knows the issues I've had with my mother-in-law, so I want to say here, for the record, that I also adored his mother. So I know it *was possible* that I could have had a mother-in-law who I actually got along with!

I really thought Sam and I would be together forever. I loved him, and he did love me, too. However (and I *hate* this "however"), a spirit told me that our having a lasting relationship wasn't to be in this lifetime. Nope, not this time. I argued with the spirits as I've done many times in my life, saying, "No! You're wrong!" We were in love. He cared about me, and he made me feel safe like no one ever had.

But the spirits said, *"Remember the love, remember the moment you're in. You have known him before and will know him again. Another time and another life."*

When Sam and I broke up, I couldn't even tell you why. It was some silly disagreement. I said to him, "You're going to meet some sixteen-year-old girl and marry her." Well, he did just that. He met a sixteen-year-old girl and five years later they were married.

I still remember the heat of a summer night, looking out a window at New York City as he lay next to me, knowing it would be the last time I would touch him in the flesh. Over the years since then, I know he thought about me. Although I never saw him again, he called me at my office number when my first book came out. His voice was exactly the same. He told me, "I thought a lot about you over these years." And certainly, I had thought about him. He said to me, "Next life is ours." The heat of summer never changes. It's always hot. I came across a poem by Wordsworth that had these lines which, for me, speak to this feeling of longing and yet acceptance, and then, beyond that, a certainty that what we shared was real and true and really will come around again in another life:

> Though nothing can bring back the hour
>
> Of splendor in the grass, of glory in the flower;
>
> We will grieve not, rather find
>
> Strength in what remains behind;
>
> In the primal sympathy
>
> Which having been must ever be;
>
> In the soothing thoughts that spring
>
> Out of human suffering;
>
> In the faith that looks through death,
>
> In years that bring the philosophic mind.

Once I became honest with myself in my twenties, I truly started
to pay attention to spirits and energy around me. When Sam and
I were no longer together, I felt I would never really love again.
So I just floated around, wasting my time, all the while hearing
spirits, but with no direction, no understanding of how to best
use this ability. Even so, I know the spirits were looking out for
me. I remember once, at around twenty-five years old, I went to a
job interview in a warehouse. Immediately upon walking in, I felt
the negative energy. I needed a job, it was close to my house, and
the hours were perfect. I met the manager and I heard: *"Run!"*
He seemed nice enough, he offered me the job, and *I ran*. On
the surface there was no reason to be nervous of this guy, but I
was placing more and more trust in what I was hearing from the
other side.

On yet another occasion, some years later, I had to take my
mother to the doctor's. I dropped her off, and the plan was that
she would call me when it was time to pick her up, because she
didn't want me to wait around for her. The doctor's office was
very close to my home in Nutley, New Jersey, so the round trip
was about ten minutes. I was back home in no time. This house
had only one entrance—it had no back door. Just as I touched
the handle to open the front door, I heard the other side saying
to me, *"Don't go in."* I had no idea what the problem was, but it
was very clear to me, and I had learned to trust the spirits. I got
back in my car and drove around the block a few times. Then I
went back again, and this time, when I went to the door, I heard
no warning. I actually was second-guessing myself, thinking that
my first reaction had been strange—I didn't know why I'd been
so nervous. Everything was fine. A little later, my mother called,
and I went and picked her up; it took me all of five minutes to
bring her home. She went into her bedroom and I heard her

gasp. I ran to see what could be the matter and was shocked to see that her whole bedroom was torn apart. We'd been robbed. I realized this meant that whoever did it had been in the house when I went to enter the first time. It really was one of the dead telling me not to go in. The robbers must have heard me and run off. They got away with $3,500, but I don't like to think of what would have happened if I had gone in while they were still there. I don't know who the soul was who gave me the warning, but they were certainly acting as my guardian angel.

Unfortunately, the other side can't save us from making mistakes. This is the side of free will. We're allowed to make our own choices here, no matter how much advice or strong suggestion we may be receiving.

I thought back to a few years earlier, when I worked at a municipal bonds place. The office manager, who I'll call "Jerry," asked me out for a drink. I was still broken inside from my breakup with Sam, and I just didn't care. So I went. We ended up in a motel, during which time I heard a spirit telling me that Jerry's wife was pregnant. He never mentioned that, of course. Apparently he did not even know it yet, and he already had three daughters.

He said, "Let's do this again."

I replied, "Go home, your wife is pregnant." He looked at me like I had three heads, but then found out it was true.

I've made mistakes—lots of them. Some make me embarrassed to think of them, and some make me ashamed. And I made all of mine with angels at my side, trying to help me. If you learn to listen, you will know that they are always trying to help you, too. In this case, before I'd even done anything I would live to regret, they said, *"Come on, Concetta, get out of here. You don't belong here."* And I did not listen. When they said Jerry's wife was expecting a baby, I could not bear another moment. The motel is still outside the Lincoln Tunnel, and, every time I see it, I'm reminded of that moment, that lesson. I was broken-hearted for years after Sam, I felt more alone than ever before in my life. When I look back on it today, I realize I was never alone. But I had lessons to learn.

A few years later, I worked as a front-desk receptionist for the second floor of a large company. (My husband, John, says I used to take calls for the second floor, now I take calls from the top floor—that is, God.) One day, a young man walked in and gave his name. I immediately heard the other side tell me that this was Sam's brother! Now, understand, Sam only had two sisters that I knew of, raised by a single mom, but I heard, *"This is Sam's brother."*

I asked him, "Do you know you have a brother and two sisters?" It turned out I was right. I put them in touch with each other and neither knew about the others. It was amazing. All my life I've had experiences like this one, "knowing," because I would hear from the dead what the real story was. As I got older, it only got more clear, and stronger. I was getting better at listening and reading the signs.

By the time I got to the age when I met John, who would become my husband, I was really aware. I knew he was an honest man and a good human being. Nothing is ever perfect on this side of the veil, so there was some baggage. But I knew he was the right one for me.

These days, I have a pretty good relationship with the other side—I know they only want to help. But sometimes I have to ask the spirits to give me a break. It's not like they are yelling, but they do clamor for my attention if I don't consciously turn it off. I could be pushing my cart through Shoprite, passing by another shopper, and I'll hear, *"Concetta! That's my daughter there!"*

I can't just go up to someone in the store and say, "Excuse me, ma'am, but your dead mother would like to tell you something." People are a lot more knowledgeable these days about the psychic, but there's still a risk of having someone call the men in white coats!

I always say—and I'll talk more about this throughout this book—that everyone has the ability to connect with the spirits of loved ones on the other side. When we sleep, our conscious mind rests and our subconscious mind becomes more heightened and aware. Over the years, I have trained my conscious mind to step back, so I can listen to my subconscious thoughts more easily, and that's the frequency where I hear the dead. It's just like any other human ability—some have it more as a natural gift, and it's at a very high level without their having to use much effort, and some may have to really work at it and it still won't be as strong as another person's. Not every swimmer can even dream of being Michael Phelps. Not every person who tries to draw, even after many art classes, will be Leonardo da Vinci. I happen to have unusually focused concentration. I don't really know how to explain it. I remember once I was having a minor surgery and the anesthesiologist told me to count while the drug took effect. I think most people would get to about "three" and—*zonk!*— they're out. I don't know how far along I was in the numbers, but I heard this guy saying to me, "Okay, you can stop counting now,

Concetta. You're asleep." Even unconscious, there was a part of me that was aware and functioning!

I also have one ear that doesn't have a hole in it, which may somehow increase my ability to focus inward, since I'm getting reduced input from the outside. This is exactly what it sounds like. No hole. That means no sound is going in on that side. It's only a theory, but it makes sense to me since I know that I need to listen in a different way from other people, and without hearing on one side I'm getting half the distraction that others must get. In any case, over the years, the way I receive impressions—hearing, seeing, feeling the spirits—has changed somewhat. Everything has become clearer, more intense, and—I feel—deeper as well. I think it's because I've been at it now professionally for twenty years. Like anything else you use or study, you get sharper.

That said, I don't have a perfect batting average. I frequently tell my clients or my audiences that I have no idea what I'm talking about. And I mean that literally! The dead on the other side know who they are talking to, and they know things that their loved one will recognize. The way I most often get myself into trouble is trying to "interpret" what they are showing or telling me, instead of just passing it along for the person here to make sense of. In one example that comes to mind, my friend Debbie's grandmother had passed. I knew her grandmother on this side and liked her a lot. But I wasn't here when she died; my husband John and I were traveling. Some time later, I saw Debbie, and all of a sudden her Nonna shows up. Nonna kept showing me an American flag.

I said, "Debbie, was Nonna ever in the military?"

Debbie said, "No! Why would you think that?"

I said, "Well, she's waving an American flag, so I thought that must be it."

Debbie said, "No, Concetta. Nonna died on Memorial Day!"

Anyone who is psychic might be psychic in a different way. Some people hear things, which is called clairaudience; some see things, which is called clairvoyance. In my case, all my senses are involved—sight, sound, touch, smell. I might smell beer and know that the spirit on the other side was a beer drinker, or smell cigar or pipe smoke and be able to tell the person I'm reading for that their loved one was a smoker, but not cigarettes, which makes it more distinctive and gives them greater assurance that this really is their own loved one. Other times, I might hear sounds or music or singing, and that's often tough for me to relay. I consider myself a pretty decent singer, but there's no karaoke machine on the other side, and sometimes I don't know the song. I just do my best. When Teresa Giudice, one of the stars of *The Real Housewives of New Jersey*, lost her mother, I was asked to help the family connect with her. I could hear a song, which fortunately I recognized and could convey to the group. It turned out it was a song her brother Joe had danced to with his mother at his wedding.

On occasion, the dead will make use of my own personal experiences in order to convey a message by association. They might show me my brother Harold, who died from AIDS, and if I then mention AIDS, lo and behold, the person I'm reading for will tell me that someone close to them passed from AIDS, and we'll know who it is who is talking. I might feel a pain or pressure in one area of the body that suggests to me how the individual passed, or I might get an emotional sense, like happy, sad, worried, or fearful, during a reading. Emotions are our internal navigation system. We are literally steered, and sometimes pushed along, by our feelings to do something or understand something. These kinds of sensations are definitely useful to me in figuring out what the spirit wants to say, but going through a lot of emotional changes in a session—or particularly a two-hour show—is very hard on me, and one of the reasons why I always pray for protection and guidance. Prayer is invaluable in my work. I ask to be filled with the love and peace of God. It gives me strength and I know I am safe.

So that's a bit about me and a bit about how I work. I've been pals with the dead a very long time now, and I hope as you read you'll get comfortable with the idea that, even if you are not a psychic medium, everyone has their folks around them, keeping tabs on them, sending comfort and any kind of help they can. Along with my brother, both my parents now are on the other side—I think of them as my own personal God Squad. You have yours, too.

Chapter 2

I Thought You Looked Familiar

All of us here on earth are spiritual beings having a physical experience. We have been spirits for eons; in human terms, we've been spirits "forever," and we have so many connections to others here, but our physical body tends to give us the illusion of separateness and keeps us from recognizing that we are all the same, all spirit, all one. I believe we have all lived before and come back to this earth many times, have lived many lives in many different places. In a sense, we are all time-travelers, even though we're mostly unaware of it.

We all experience being different genders, races, social and economic classes, and religions. We will experience being both the innocent and the guilty, the accuser and the accused, the betrayer and the betrayed, the punisher and the rescuer, the "haves" and the "have-nots." We will learn how it feels to be on the receiving end, and we'll learn we have a choice to show kindness. We get to see how each of those things feels. There's so much we need to learn, so much this plane of struggle has to teach us. How much could we experience and learn in just one single lifetime? If we care about improving ourselves, becoming better and more pure in spirit, growing ever closer to God, then reincarnation—that is, many chances to learn—just makes so much sense.

Everything is made of energy, and energy never dies. Everything in nature is recycled. Trees and plants die, go back to the earth, and sprout again. We recycle paper, plastic, glass, and all kinds of material goods. And souls, the spirits within each of us, are no exception; they get recycled too. Anything that is created by God goes back to God; no life is destroyed. This is the understanding in many, many religions and cultures all around the world. Even the Pope has said this!

In my early teens, I had memories of myself holding a microphone in my hand, singing. I felt the stage that I once stood on. In the introduction to this book, I told the story of a time when I was five and supposed to perform a rendition of "How Much Is that Doggie in the Window" with a group of other little girls, but instead did a diva turn, waiting until they were done to sing it on my own. A ham was born! I knew I was supposed to be there, because I had memories of being an entertainer. All my life, I struggled to understand what I was supposed to do. *How do I get there? Who do I call?* Throughout my school years, I settled for being the class clown and putting on kiddie shows in the neighborhood, and later I put on holiday shows at office parties. I even got up at family weddings to tell jokes—at eleven years old, that is really brave!

When I was in my twenties, I worked as a receptionist for Givaudan, a company that makes fragrances and flavors. I loved working there—it was such a fancy place that my reception desk was as big as a Bentley! Every day, they would bring a huge new arrangement of fresh-cut flowers; I really felt in my element. Beyond my desk, a couple of steps down, was a beautifully appointed salon, like an atrium with windows, high ceilings, and fancy couches and chairs where visitors would wait for their appointments. At Christmastime, they would bring in a tree that seemed to me to rival the one at Rockefeller Center—enormous, with unbelievable decorations and different every year. One day around the holidays, they had just finished decorating the tree, and I hadn't yet had a chance to check it out. I was waiting for another girl to relieve me so I could go to lunch with a couple of my friends. They were already there and had gone down to give the tree a closer look, oohing and ahhing over the decorations, going, "Oh my God, Concetta, you have got to see this!" So, as soon as the other girl got there, I left my desk and started down the couple steps toward them. The sun was shining very brightly through the high windows, and the tree glittered like it was on fire! As I was stepping down, I was momentarily blinded and stumbled before catching myself, but, in that split second, instead of seeing before me the tree and my couple of girlfriends, I saw an audience full of people, all dressed in 1800s evening wear! I was on stage, the lights flickering around me—I could tell that the lights were candles, not electric—and, rather than stumbling down the steps of an office building waiting area, I was taking a deep curtsy in front of an adoring standing ovation! It was incredibly vivid and real to me, but as a twenty-six-year-old I didn't want my friends to think I was a cuckoo-bird, so I never said a word about what I had seen. They were saying, "Are you all right?" and in my head I thought, *What the hell just happened???*

Years later, but still before I went public as a psychic medium, I visited a bookstore in Wayne, New Jersey, called Wise Man Books, where they used to have various metaphysical practitioners visit and do workshops or demonstrations or readings of different kinds. There was a fellow from England who was doing past-life regressions, and I did a session with him. During the regression, I talked about a life I had had as an actress in Chicago. I remembered having two husbands and I told the practitioner that both were deceased. Apparently, while under, my manner of speaking was pretty coarse and unpleasant, so my impression is that I was not the nicest person (in plain English, I seemed to be a miserable bitch), even if I got raves when I performed! I suspect my recalled standing ovation was from this same lifetime.

As a medium, many folks ask me about past lives. We've all had that experience of meeting someone and already knowing how we feel about them. We just click instantly, or the opposite. We know right away this person isn't our cup of tea, even though we haven't yet learned anything about them. Or sometimes it's a matter of knowing you haven't met them before, but something about them (their appearance or their mannerisms) is *so* familiar. Sometimes it's something pretty magical.

My friend Rachel's granddaughter turned one recently, and I was at the birthday party. (I have talked about Rachel before—she owns one of my favorite restaurants in Boonton, New Jersey, an Italian place called Top of the Park.) At the party, I was introduced to one of her brothers-in-law, Vincent, and, when he was told what I did for a living, he asked, "Can I ask you a question?"

I said, "Sure."

"What do you think," he said, "of the fact that when I was four years old, I met my wife, and I knew she was mine and I was going to marry her? What do you think of that?" (And, by the way, these two have been married now fifty years.)

I said, "I believe you 100 percent."

This is not the first time I've heard something like that. I was recalling specifically a man who came to me who told me about meeting his wife when she was only seven years old, and he was only ten. He said he knew that he'd known her before. He'd felt an electrical charge, like static electricity, when the two of them stood side by side as children. Years later, they met again, when she was twenty and he was twenty-four. He told me it was like he knew he was supposed to wait for her until the time was right. When they met again as young adults, they married and had children. Yet in spite of all this, when she died, he came to see me as a non-believer! However, when his wife showed up in my reading, she soon put him right! The first thing she said was, "I've loved you many lifetimes, and there are more to come."

Thinking about this story, I asked Vincent to tell me his.

He told me that, when he was four, the neighbors, with whom his family was friendly, had a new baby. He remembered walking into the house as a very young boy and looking at this new baby girl. He said, "Concetta, when I looked at her, I knew she was mine. I knew we'd be together for the rest of our lives. I was only four, but as we grew up, I remembered this, I knew it." They got married when she was nineteen and he was twenty-three. He gestured to his wife and said, "There she is, over there. And I love her more than anything. I loved her from the first moment I saw her, when she was a baby." These kinds of stories always make me feel so wonderful because they are proof that there is so much more going on here than we understand.

Many, many people have had the experience of meeting someone and feeling that strong connection or *zing!* of energy that we tend to call love at first sight. In the case of this man, when he felt that even as a child, he knew it signified an important connection.

When my husband John and I were traveling in Austria a couple of years ago, one of our favorite stops was Salzburg. This town was simply intoxicating with the energy of its history. Everything is beautifully preserved. It's just absolutely gorgeous, and there seems to be music everywhere, which makes sense since Mozart was born there.

We took a tram ride up to the top of a high hill to see Hohensalzburg Fortress. This "white castle" (not to be confused with the hamburger chain) is actually where the town gets its name, as "Salzburg" means "salt fortress." As we walked to the tram, we passed very old cemeteries that were just incredible. I love old European cemeteries, and in these the graves were decorated with lovely figures and statues; some had fancy iron gates with elaborate writing on them. I wished I could read the different languages, but as I stood in front of different graves, I could feel the stories of the lives the individuals had lived. I had the feeling I had known many of them sometime, somewhere in the past.

As we wandered the cobblestone streets, taking in all the quaint little shops, I was drawn to one that had a table with an array of handmade Jewish treasures, mostly jewelry, some beaded bracelets, with the Star of David and other Jewish motifs, but also some beautiful scarves. Everything else in the store was made in Austria, but the items on this table were made in Israel. As I got to talking with the shop owner, I expressed my curiosity about these things, asking her why she was featuring these Jewish pieces from Israel. "Oh," she said with a sweet smile, "I know it might seem strange, but all my life I've had memories of seeing Jewish people in camps. I see German uniforms. Sometimes I'm frightened, and sometimes I feel very angry. I'm not sure what role I may have played in a past life, but I know I took part in this. I'm not Jewish, but it's become my passion to love the Jewish faith and people."

I completely understood, as I, too, believe I was Jewish in a past life, and have written in a previous book about my experience visiting Dachau, feeling the powerful negativity that still exists there.

Frequently when I'm doing a reading for one of my Jewish clients, the subject of a Bar Mitzvah or Bat Mitzvah will come up, and I always feel a tickle of love picturing the community gathering for these special events. The first time I heard a Jewish person go "Poo poo poo" after talking about something they hoped for, I just "knew" exactly what it meant. (For the uninitiated, it's basically meant to be spitting three times to ward off the evil eye that might jinx a good outcome.) If these felt connections were not enough, there's also the time my friend John Cornick invited me to his mother's house for Seder. Now I'm Italian and we love our food—at an Italian dinner, the bread basket hits the table before anyone's butt hits their chair! So imagine my surprise at seeing a handful of herbs, a hard-boiled egg, and some dry crackers (matzo)—the only thing that looked a little promising was the kugel! But once the prayers were being said and one of the guests was retelling the story of the Jewish exodus out Egypt where they had been slaves, I could feel the tears streaming down my face, like this was the story of my own people.

More recently, I had a dream where I looked down at my arms and they were totally emaciated. Somehow I knew it was 1942 and I was struggling with whether or not I could actually make it to the end of the war. It was so vivid and definitely from a past life.

If we are paying attention, we all have had instances where we become aware that we have "been here before" on the earth plane. There may be a particular historical period that we feel a connection to—a passion for learning about ancient Egypt or Greece, or feeling drawn to Civil War sites or reenactments. There may be certain music that is from well before our time that we just love hearing, or we love paintings or novels from a particular period. Someone who grew up in the Midwest may feel drawn to New York City's deep skyscraper canyons, or yearn to hear waves crashing on a beach, never knowing where these inclinations come from. Our past lives can also show themselves in irrational fears we have in this life, like a fear of heights or of water, when we have never had an experience in this lifetime that would suggest that either of these posed a particular danger to us.

When I was about eighteen or nineteen years old, I knew a girl about my age who was gorgeous and popular, very feet-on-the-ground and normal in every way, except that she was completely petrified of blood. Her aversion was so strong that it definitely seemed irrational. If she saw blood, she had a very strong reaction, as if she was having a panic attack, but even if she just heard about an accident or someone getting cut, she reacted with terror, like she was watching a horror movie. I remember knowing there was something else going on. I wasn't as up to speed then as I am now, but I sensed even then that it had something to do with the other side, a past life. This poor girl was experiencing violent "memories" from deep in her subconscious; something happening to her or someone she cared about in a life she'd lived before this one. I knew her family and who was around her—there was nothing in this life that would be a cause of such an extreme reaction. But what I can tell you is that I also used to see spirits around her—a grandfather in particular—asking me to help her. I'm sorry to say that I wasn't yet up to the task. I was still trying to understand my ability and what I could and could not do. But it gives me a lot of hope that I know she had guardians who cared about her and were looking for any means they could find to comfort her.

Sometimes knowing we have been here before is just a feeling of, "I fit perfectly here." One of my friends grew up on a farm in Pennsylvania—it wasn't even "small-town," it was rural, and her family kept horses. But she always had an attraction to New York City and always felt she needed to go there. Nobody in her family lived there, or *had* lived there, at least no family member she was aware of. She went to New York when she was twenty and she never left. For her it was home, very possibly because she had lived there before.

The ex-husband of a good friend of mine moved to Thailand and found happiness again with a Thai woman. He said that is where he feels at home and the best he's ever felt; he's at peace. It's something that he never felt living in the United States, even though he was born here. After visiting Thailand once, he sold everything he had here and moved. He said he is the happiest he's ever been. He believes that he lived there before, in a past life.

We can get a lot of information about our past lives through recurring dreams. Not every dream we have more than once will point to a past life—there are definitely those that have more to do with our worries in this lifetime or may be set off by something that happened to us in our childhood and so forth. But, very frequently, the dreams that come back to us over and over and show us in places that we may vaguely remember, or stir strong emotions in us, or for which we just have no reasonable explanation, can be hints at a past life. I've had many clients share these kinds of dreams with me.

I recall one client, a woman in her sixties who was Italian through and through, both sides of the family. She told me she could relate to everything Italian. The black hair, the black Italian grandmother shoes, she spoke Italian, she probably carried garlic around in her pocket. As far as she knew, there was not a drop of anything else in her blood. But for some reason she had recurring dreams with bagpipe music, green mountainsides, and people wearing clothes that she felt were from the 1700s. She vaguely associated these things with Ireland, where she had never gone and had not even much interest in. She'd had these dreams for years, being only mildly curious about them. Recently, however, her niece had gotten interested in genealogy and had researched the family tree. She came to find out that a couple centuries ago, they'd had a number of family members who had come from Scotland! Now, of course, she can't help wondering if her dreams are actually half-formed memories from a past life she once lived.

Another client that comes to mind was a new one I'll call "Laura." I did not know her at all, but she appeared to be a wealthy woman and told me she was married to a municipal bond dealer. As I did her reading, I kept hearing what sounded like American Indian chanting. I saw what I recognized as the canyons of the West. Laura said she never had gone west; however, she did admit to a dream she'd had many times in her life. She said in her dream she was walking on the dry desert floor, carrying a basket and looking for vegetation. And she'd had other dreams with similar images. She'd never thought much about the dreams until her daughter was born. As her daughter started to talk, she said things that made no sense to Laura. Her daughter was attracted to Indian dolls, and, when she was five, she asked to dress as an Indian princess for Halloween. As a young child, Laura's daughter asked questions like, "Why do we live *here* now?" The home they were in was the only one she had known in her five years, so Laura was confused by the question. When she asked what her daughter meant, her daughter told her that she'd liked "the other house" better. (One room of their home where her daughter did seem very comfortable was the family room, which Laura had decorated in the colors and motifs of the Southwest, just because she'd always liked them even though she'd never lived there.) Laura said she offered to get her daughter a puppy, but her daughter insisted she wanted a horse. She would talk about missing people by name, none of whom Laura knew and some whose names she couldn't pronounce or remember. One her daughter mentioned numerous times was "Yellow Flower." Laura and her husband did get a dog for their daughter (unfortunately, they didn't live in an area where they could have a horse) and they named the dog "Flower." Laura asked me if she and her daughter might have had another life together as Native Americans. I had the sense that Laura was looking for confirmation of what she already believed—that her dreams and her daughter's vivid memories really were from a past life. She wanted permission to accept the truth of this. I encouraged Laura to trust her own feelings and her daughter's and to nurture her daughter's affinity for horses and Native American history, maybe take her to places where she can learn more about it. Whatever role each of them played in that lifetime, to give it consideration now is worthwhile. Never forget that we are all one, and our multiple lives are intended to show us the full range of human experiences and let us deal with any karma we have accumulated. Having an awareness of a past life is a blessing. It can support your spiritual growth in this lifetime, because just knowing these lives are something you personally experienced can increase your empathy.

Another client I recall, a sweet older woman, told me about her beloved five-year-old grandson, with whom she was very close. It was clear that the boy favored her over his other grandparents, and the family always teased her about spoiling him. This all sounds very normal and sweet. However, she was coming to me for a particular reason that she wouldn't tell her family because she feared their reaction. She wasn't looking to hear from her husband who had passed; rather, she wanted to know if I believed in past lives. Her grandson had confided to her that he had known her before.

One day, the little grandson asked my client where Sarah was. She was puzzled because she didn't know any Sarah. But, because she had such a special relationship with the boy, she played along.

She said, "Honey, I don't know where she is."

And the boy continued with information. He asked, "Is she at Moffy's house?"

Moffy is a strange name, so that made the woman even more curious. She asked the boy more questions. She asked, "Do you love Sarah?" I thought this was brilliant. Instead of asking, "Who's Sarah?"

The boy said, "Oh yes, Grandma, she's my wife!" You can imagine my client's amazement at that point. Finally, she asked who Moffy was. Her grandson looked confused and said, "Sarah's mommy!" The icing on the cake was when he said, "Grandma, you were there too. You lived in the stone house." After that, she talked with the boy a number of times about this life he apparently remembered before coming here this time. He would never talk about it in front of others, and she noticed that, as he got older and she'd ask him questions, he'd begin to just say that he didn't remember.

For some reason, the age of five seems a little magical for children having these kinds of memories, whether of who and where they were before, or sometimes in remembering details of their transition back to this plane. I think this is possibly because, by the age of five, kids have enough vocabulary and insight to be able to communicate these things verbally, but still have at least some connection to those lives, which tend to disappear the older we get.

For example, one morning, my stepdaughter Jessica was combing her daughter Isabella's hair when Isabella was around five years old. Out of the blue, Isabella said, "I'm glad I picked you to be my mommy."

Jessica thought this was so cute, so she played along, saying, "Why is that?"

Isabella said, "I saw you first. You were in a restaurant with Daddy and you looked so pretty and so nice. I saw another lady, and they asked me if I wanted to go with her, but I said no. I picked you."

Jessica said, "Is that right? Well, what restaurant did you see us in? Do you remember?"

Isabella said, "I don't know what restaurant it was. But it had a lot of fish swimming around near where you were sitting."

With that, Jessica went from having an amusing conversation with her daughter to being really shocked. There was a restaurant she and her husband used to go to very frequently in the town they lived in before Isabella was born, and it did have a large fish tank, like a wall of glass, that separated areas of the dining room.

After she was born, they moved, so they had not been back to that restaurant since Isabella was a tiny baby.

As I told my client, *I know reincarnation is real.* We all move back and forth, from spiritual to physical, and back again. It's clear that her grandson did indeed know her before. I told her that the boy was just beginning to put his focus where it should be now—on this lifetime. As soon as we grow from childhood we begin to adhere to this side of the veil, to our present lives on the physical plane, and become more preoccupied with material things. With everything that ordinary life demands of us, it's no wonder we choose to focus here, now. This is normal. It would be really confusing if we had awareness of all our lifetimes simultaneously and had to consciously work out all of them at the same time. But we still have those connections, faint memories, feelings, unexplainable connections, likes or dislikes, or simply interests that we can't explain. *Why* are we interested?

One thing that a lot of people seem to be confused about is that they think reincarnation is a punishment. We've done something wrong, so we have to come back and fix it. There is certainly an element of "correction" to our multiple lives, a balancing of our karma, but I think of it more as an opportunity to learn and grow spiritually. Nobody is "born bad," we are born with karmic situations that we need to try to work our way through. Sometimes we come back in relationship to a soul we've had dealings with before, where one or the other (or both) has the chance to do better than the last time. Having an awareness that this is not the only life we've lived gives us an opportunity to do some reflecting. Like the woman in Austria who was uncertain about her role during the Holocaust, but whose memories made her uneasy, we might want to look for ways we can be proactive about healing our past actions. Even if we were not "evil" in a past life, none of us was perfect either. And frankly, none of us has been perfect in this current life we're living. We all have things we regret and would like to make amends for. As long as we are still living, there is time to wake up and smell the coffee (and the donuts, too, if we are lucky).

Throughout our lives, our senses are really important— they ignite something in our souls. I recently found myself contemplating a different sort of smell than coffee and donuts, one I recalled from my childhood. What smell was it? Horse manure.

I had a memory of being about eight years old. Where I grew up was in the countryside, but in a residential area, not on a farm. It wasn't like "the country" of a hundred years ago, but still pretty rustic compared to what this area looks like now. I remember there was a farmhouse nearby, and in this memory I was walking with a bunch of little kids to investigate the barn. And I remember the smell of manure. Believe it or not, as I remember this, to me it was more than just the smell of manure with a bunch of little kids going "Ew—horse shit!" I remember the smell relating to a time, maybe in the 1700s or 1800s, when probably the scent of manure permeated everything because that's what we used in our lives—animals, horses—for every kind of work and conveyance. And I remember, as a child, that smell ignited memories in my soul that had to do with other times, outside of being in the 1960s and walking around with some friends. It made me think about how different scents hold memories for us—walking into a house and thinking, *Oh, this smells like my grandmother's house,* or smelling a fragrance on someone that you associate with someone you loved and having it release wonderful warm memories. Sometimes we are addicted to a certain scent, and we smell it in passing and just want more of it because it reminds us of something pleasant. I'm sure there's an adverse side to that too, that certain scents can repel us because of old memories we relate to them. But I can tell you that, for me, the scent of manure stirs up feelings and sense memories that have to do with past lives, knowing I lived in times when there was no running water or bath facilities. I don't have a negative reaction to that scent. I actually find myself wanting to prolong it, to stay and continue to smell it, because somewhere in this are some very warm loving memories.

Last night I was watching *Outlander* on TV and I was thinking, at my age, I can't believe all the changes that have taken place in the short amount of time I've lived on earth. How many things have changed, just in the little town I live in? There's been so much growth, so many new people. And so much change around the world, too, of course. It's been going on since the beginning of time. It's so amazing how far we've come. The one thing that hasn't changed is that people are still looking for the "answer" to life and death. People still want to know, "What's it like to die?" "Where do we go when we die?" "What's it like on the other side?" "Will I come back here again?" "And who will I be if I do?" These same questions have been asked for thousands of years and are still being asked today.

I am now in my sixties, and I ponder the experiences in my life, my actions, things I said and did, and what I have learned. I think about what I could do better, and what I'd like to be able to do over. I sometimes think about words I'd like to take back. I am well aware of my own past lives and past behavior, and often I'll add a line to my nighttime prayers: "Please forgive my past sins and poor choices—and the sins and poor choices of my past lives."

Chapter 3

A Catholic, a Muslim, and a Jew Walk into a Bar

In spite of the fact that this world seems to be broken up into many different pieces, that is, lots of different beliefs and religions, there is just one God for all people, so we all need to share. I believe God is for us all—good, bad, or indifferent. Everyone here is on their own path, dealing with karma from other lifetimes, dealing with lessons in this lifetime. They may be digging themselves out of a deep spiritual hole or falling into one. They may be dealing with issues we have no knowledge or understanding of. Even though we're human and often can't help ourselves, it's not for us to judge.

The best I can tell is that religion is basically a tool for our spiritual growth. Within each religion, we learn lessons according to the sacred texts belonging to that religion, and the funny thing is that there is a great deal of overlap among them. I would say that, in those various texts, there is some stuff that doesn't seem like it belongs there, because maybe it contradicts the overall message of love and acceptance, but we probably need to chalk that up to "human error." After all, God did not actually write the Bible, for example, men did. And they may have gotten a few things wrong, just like when I listen for a message from a client's dead loved one—I'm certainly doing my best and my heart's in the right place, but I'm not 100 percent perfect. I do a pretty good job, but I can sometimes misunderstand what I'm being told, and so, even though I'll tell my client what I believe I'm getting, it could be a little off. *We are human!*

But besides the lessons that are directly in the texts we study under our various religions, religion is also a tool for growth in another way because of the very differences between them. The fact that they do diverge on some points gives us a huge opportunity to learn to love *in spite of our differences.* I have family members of different ethnicities and faiths, and I meet wonderful folks everywhere I go of many different religions, and I have found that the common thread among them all is trusting in God and treating all others as you would like to be treated yourself—really simple Golden Rule stuff. We are all looking for the same things: love, compassion, forgiveness, and hope. And each of us can choose how we reach out to and interact with others who we think are not like ourselves.

I remember being around ten years old, playing with another girl my age who was Jewish. I did not really understand what that meant. I only had been told by someone that people of her religion did not believe that Jesus was their savior. But my parents accepted all differences, so I did too. Unknowingly, as I went into her home, I could feel the goodness in the energy in the home.

(I want to say, as an aside here, that I don't think this type of experience is something that only a psychic medium could have. Nearly all of us have had similar experiences in our friends' homes. Think back to when you were a kid, visiting with a playmate. When you went into the house, if the father or mother was mean, you felt it, right? You could feel it in the very air if there was abuse going on in that home. We all have this "sensitivity" to these emotional vibrations. On the other hand, if kindness prevailed, we would know that, too. When we're young, we have fewer filters, so our sensitivity is at an all-time high. We develop filters—or protective layers—as we get older, thinking, perhaps subconsciously, that they'll keep us safe.)

Religion has always been a touchy subject. I always imagine God shaking his beautiful head at us all. I myself have dealt with religious differences among family members.

When my brother Harold died, I'd been married for seven years. Three of my in-laws came to the wake. I will only say that they walked in like Joan Collins from the show *Dynasty*. Yes, they showed up, but I felt no empathy from them. Two days after Harold's burial was Palm Sunday. A command performance was expected at my mother-in-law's home for dinner. I was deeply upset and heartbroken and not wanting to go, but I felt the pressure and did not want to rock the boat. Disoriented, as anyone would be who had lost someone so dear to them just a short time before, I walked into a celebration of Jesus. But there was none of his compassion there. We had buried Harold just days before, but no one mentioned my brother's name. At all. No one asked me how I was, no one gave me an understanding hug, no one made a point to show me any kindness or love. I sat across from John's grandmother and one of his sisters-in-law, both of whom were laughing and whispering, giving me dirty looks. It's hard to believe anyone could be this cold—I was horrified. I could not imagine treating anyone in this manner, let alone on Holy Sunday. I've watched many times some folks go to church on Sunday, get their forehead streaked with ashes on Ash Wednesday, set out a big Christmas dinner, and so much more, but then treat their fellow human beings with utter disregard.

On the other hand, my mother, in spite of terrible treatment she had received from nuns in a Catholic orphanage, never held onto anger or hate. Knowing what she went through, I said, "I hate those nuns! How could God allow that?"

But she would say, "It wasn't God, it was frustrated women. God didn't make them do that—it was a choice they made. God is good."

We are all born with a moral compass, but our life experiences can twist our understanding of right and wrong and how to treat others. Frequently, those who were abused become abusers themselves. My mother was one of the strongest people I've ever known. Whatever she went through, she was always able to hold onto a higher vision of herself, not as someone who wanted to get even, but someone who just practiced love.

My family was a mix of Catholic and Protestant. Both my parents told my siblings and me that we could make the decision of what religion we wanted to follow for ourselves, and they would respect it, enjoy it, and *love* it.

I had a client come to see me, a nice man who was Jewish and married to a Catholic woman. The couple had three children and raised them in his wife's religion. But his mother was furious with him and made it known in every way possible. Besides persistent disparaging comments, she also refused to take part in any sort of religious celebration—Christmas versus Hanukkah was an especially sore spot. The fact that he didn't bring his kids up Jewish caused a great deal of grief between mother and son, and, when she passed, he was miserable. He felt so guilty. None of this he told me. But as I sat with this gentleman, I heard his mother immediately. She opened with, "Tell my son that God is real. It's all the same; God is for everyone. I'm sorry, I'm sorry." As I related to him what his mother was saying, he sat staring at me before he revealed the backstory on his mother's comments. He was so happy, and I could literally feel the love and joy filling my office. Then his mother said, "Send my love to June," his wife. "Say I am sorry." Many more details were given to validate his mother's presence in the room, and he left with a greater sense of peace than he had known in a long while.

We separate ourselves from others because of fear. And most of our fear stems from a lack of understanding. When I started hearing about terrorist attacks, especially after 9/11, I built up a tremendous fear of Muslims. I was not proud of myself, but this is the truth. But I am a huge Dunkin' Donuts fan, and there's one in Boonton that I go to all the time. I noticed that first there was one young Muslim girl working there, then a second one appeared. Then, soon after, it seemed like most of the counter staff and the manager appeared to be Muslim. All the young women had their hair covered and no makeup. As I've said, the truth is, this made me feel nervous. But I try not to live my life in fear, I try to be respectful of everyone, and these people certainly had done nothing to me. So here I come...the big blonde hair, bright red lipstick, all my blingy jewelry. And I'm true to my personality, very chatty and upbeat.

After a while, the girls began to recognize me and to tease me about my coffee order. I take my coffee super light, with ten or twelve pumps of half-and-half. And then a little later, they began to compliment me, making little comments like "Oh, I love your lipstick," "Your hair looks so nice," "I really love your necklace." They really seemed to love all the fun, feminine touches I enjoy wearing so much. Our connection really made me think about religious expression. If I can wear a cross or a Star of David (both of which I do), then why shouldn't they wear something that indicates their religious beliefs? Everyone should be entitled. It did make me feel good that we could have fun together, exchanging little jokes, and I really started to like all of them.

Then, one day, there was a new girl working there, and, when I came up to the counter, she asked me for my order. Before I could say anything, one of the regulars jumped in. "She likes it super light. Like her!" I thought that was funny and cute. I said, "That's right! Super light, like me!"

I say this all the time: I could not do the work I do without the help of God and those who are in His light. Any time I am doing a reading or a show, I first have to pray for His protection, and I tell any negative spirits that are not in the light that they are simply not welcome. So I feel perfectly comfortable saying that I could not do this work without God's permission and blessing. There are still those who don't understand, or even fear, the psychic, and very frequently—and sadly—it's religion that gets in the way. Sometimes people let their religion stand between them and something that could give them comfort or make them happy.

One example of this was the mother-in-law of a good friend's son, who is a born-again Christian. It's part of her religion to try to get everyone to convert to it, even though they might be very happy with the religion they already have. Frankly, it drives everybody crazy. When her husband died, she missed him very much, but refused to believe that he might be able to communicate with her. She just refused. Anything my friend suggested she try, she shot it down. But still my friend, from time to time, would encourage her to keep her eyes open, and tell her that she might get a message from her husband.

One day, this woman was walking on the beach near her home and saw a heart drawn in the sand that said, "I love you, Matt." Matt was her husband's name! The heart was above the waterline, so no waves had washed it, but also there were no footprints around it. She told this story to my friend, her daughter's mother-in-law, but the moment my friend suggested that it was her deceased husband sending her a message, she got very angry and said absolutely not, that would be the work of the Devil!

I just don't see how people can believe this. In my world, God is much stronger!

In another story that comes to mind, I had a guy come to the house who was going to fix a dented rim on our car. He actually made house calls, and he was very nice, smiling and friendly. My office has a separate entrance, so that people coming for a reading don't have to go through the house, and, when he saw the sign, he said, "Oh, 'Concetta Bertoldi,' what do you do? Are you a decorator?" Once I told him what I did, his whole demeanor changed. He all but crossed himself, giving me a pretty horrible look. His look seemed to say, *Yeah lady, I'll fix your tire. But you just keep your distance from me.* We were still the same two people who had just met and exchanged pleasantries with big smiles on our faces. But, just that fast, everything was different. I have a very hard time understanding the judgments some people make, but try to bear in mind that when we come back here to the earth plane we all are arriving at various points in our spiritual progress, and we also may have been, in a way, indoctrinated, in our upbringing or through our experiences, to have particular beliefs. I myself, as I've just described, have struggled not to form preconceived notions about people, so I try to keep this in mind. It ain't easy for any of us here on the earth plane!

I try to live my life in the light of God at all times, and it's natural for me to feel that energy all around me. But there are some places that really are special and seem to magnify the feeling. For example, several years ago, I went on a girls' trip to Italy with my friends Mushy and Debbie (I'll say more about this trip in a later chapter). One day, toward the end of our trip, Mushy was doing some tidying up, getting ready for our return, and Debbie and I went to see an old church. I cannot now recall the name of the church; it was just a beautiful old Catholic cathedral. Debbie and I had visited other churches on other trips, but we'd never sat through an entire mass in a foreign country before, and this one was all in Latin. Knowing some Italian, we were able to pick out a word here or there, but, for the most part, the sound of the words just rolled over us. Even not understanding what was being said, it was one of the most beautiful services I've ever heard. The energy, the love on people's faces. We were in a place where we could feel the Holy Spirit truly lived. When we got up to say, "God be with you," everyone greeted us. It was just very moving. I mention this to say that, even though this was a Catholic service, it could have as easily been a Jewish service or a Muslim service. It was really the energy of God and the sense that all of us were one.

Chapter 4

I Know What You Did Last Summer

There's one question I've heard so frequently in my career. It's
been asked in all different ways. I started bringing it up at my
shows as an icebreaker—if someone in the audience didn't beat
me to it—and it always makes the house both laugh and cringe.
It even became the title of my first book: *Do Dead People Watch
You Shower?* I'm not sure why everybody wants to know this.
I guess it can feel pretty creepy to think that, no matter where
you go, your deceased grandparents, parents, great aunts and
uncles, et cetera, are watching you. But here's the answer to that
question: *They sure do!* There is literally, my friend, nowhere to
hide. Wherever you go, there they are!

If knowing this freaks you out, I hope it'll make you feel better
when I tell you that they are only watching over you with your
best interests in mind. If they happen to see you in the shower,
it's not in the sense of a Peeping Tom. They don't care; they are
not in human form. They remember their human lives, but they
don't relate to it in the same way anymore. As spirit, they judge
nothing. They want only your happiness.

And, once they are on the other side, they could not care less
about settling any scores. They understand the reason behind
anything that happened to them here. They understand if
someone hurt them unintentionally, and they forgive if someone
hurt them intentionally for any human reason. They understand
it was an error, a poor choice, and that the other person will have
to find a way to correct their own behavior.

Every week, for the last decade or so, someone has come in to my
office worried that a dead loved one on the other side is still mad
at them about something they said or did when their loved one
was alive. I see it so often, I almost printed up T-shirts: "They're
Over It. But Are You?" Nobody over there is mad, and it saddens

me to see so much pain and suffering here, when all the spirits tell me that love is the emotion that makes it to the other side. Even the most heartbreaking vendettas can be wiped away after someone gets to the other side.

A couple of years ago, a journalist was in town to interview me after one of my live events. She joined my husband John and me for dinner afterward, and as, we were sitting there talking and eating rigatoni, I saw a man standing behind her. He felt like grandfather energy.

"Do you have a grandfather on the other side?" I asked.

"I do," she said.

I looked at his spirit, and he communicated to me that he was very sorry. Apparently, he was the type of person who held a grudge when he was alive. He also tried to pit certain family members against each other. He lived for conflict and left this world with many enemies.

"He's saying to me that none of the things that he thought mattered really matter," I said. "He's very sorry he caused so much pain. He sees how he hurt people. He wants to be sure you let the family know that he understands why they might not want to hear from him, even through a medium."

The journalist's eyes widened.

"Yeah, he was a pretty mean guy," she said. "I'll have to let his children know. Some of them are still not talking to each other because of the things he did."

Her grandfather's spirit showed me that he could see all the angst that he caused and all the sadness. It was a ripple effect that he'd had to watch over and over in his life review of past actions. For those who may be unfamiliar, when we die, our soul experiences something of an instant replay of the events of the life just completed. This is where we feel everything that we put into motion when we were alive, whether positive or negative—it plays out like a movie. So, if you lived a wonderful life, if you did your best and treated others kindly, your movie will be fabulous. If you were a real jerk, then that sucker's going to be hard to watch! It's my understanding that we actually feel the damage we have done to others and experience emotions of remorse. We also experience strong feelings of love, joy, and warmth for our beautiful connections with others.

"He says that he's sorry for what he did after the reunion," I said. I didn't know what the heck he was talking about, but he was very clear that this was something I needed to say.

"Oh my gosh!" she gasped. I saw her eyes start to well up. "He didn't talk to his son, my dad, for seven years after a family reunion. It was a battle of 'he said, she said' and he chose to shut out his son over a silly misunderstanding. It broke my dad. I don't know if he ever got over it."

"He says he's with your dad now, and they've made up," I said. Apparently her dad was also on the other side because, just then, another male energy spirit appeared next to the grandfather and they were arm in arm.

"Oh, I'm so glad to hear that!" she said. "I had always wondered if they were together, and if they could put all that behind them after all was said and done."

After the journalist returned home, she told me that she relayed the message to her family.

"Most of the people in my family were so excited to hear that my grandpa and my dad were together on the other side and had mended fences," she said. "But, I have to tell you, my one aunt still won't hear it. She would rather stay mad. She's just not letting it go."

We all have stories that are similar. But the amazing thing about being in the light on the other side is that it's all about forgiveness. There are no grudges. It's beyond anything we can understand. The dead tell me that there is nobody standing there with a clipboard saying, "You really were a jerk when you were a senior in high school!" They say that, in the light, there is only love. No judgment. We judge here. There, we see how we treated others, we get a greater understanding of why it all happened, and in the end, there is only love. For those who are still on this side, the things that were left unsaid can cause a burden of guilt that hangs over us like a cloud of doom. And we can be stubborn about letting that guilt go—we want to hang on to it like we *own* it—like a brooch that people decide to pin on their jacket. We beat ourselves up with the "shoulda-woulda-couldas," the "if only I hads," or, "if only I hadn'ts."

What people don't realize is that it's just as easy to *unpin* it and take it off. But you have to be willing to do it. It's a choice to hold on to that guilt. That's part of free will. But every single person I've met in my work holds on to some sort of pin of guilt.

Even mediums.

When I was twenty-seven years old, I was one smoking hot tamale. I'll be honest—I had it going on. I mean, now, things have gone south for the winter and I look like a map of Italy. But back then, I was a force to be reckoned with.

There was this guy, I'll call him "Mark," and he was in love with me. And I knew he was nuts about me and I would let him take me out, but I wasn't really into him.

One day, he asked me to go to a wedding with him, so I said, "Yeah, I'll go." At the time, I didn't have anything better to do, so why not?

And it's funny because he kept asking me, "Are you sure?" It's almost like he knew.

Sadly, something more appealing came along, and I didn't go to the wedding. But I didn't let him know this. I just didn't answer the phone all day. I was horrible to this poor guy. Even now, I feel so awful that I did this. It was a really mean thing to do. This is one of my *pins of guilt* that I choose to carry around on my lapel. I know that what I did was so wrong. This is what we humans do to punish ourselves when we know we weren't acting in integrity: We hold on to the guilt.

Years later, I saw him one night when I was out with my husband, John. We were at some fancy place, and I walked up to him. I wasn't sure what I was going to do, but I thought facing the music would be better than walking in the other direction. As I approached him, the look of disdain that he shot my way felt like someone hit me in the stomach with a baseball bat. He didn't say a word, but his eyes said, *Forget about* you, *lady.* And I deserved every bit of that anger. I had it coming. He walked away from me, and when I tried to find him later that evening, he was gone. I truly regret the fact that I never got to apologize.

But the incident with Mark isn't the only screwup on my resume. I also got busted for shoplifting.

Whoops!

Let me set the stage: When I was in my twenties, I was in a shop called Bradley's with another girl, and I was buying a pair of jeans. Now, at that time, the popular perfume was *Lauren* by Ralph Lauren. I had a shopping cart that had these big gaps in it, so I put the small perfume bottle in the pocket of the jeans I was going to try on, just so it wouldn't fall on the floor. So, when I went to put the jeans on, the perfume was already in the pocket, and I thought *Hmmm...who's gonna know?*

"You're gonna know, Concetta."

The spirits—my better angels—were trying to get through, but I just pushed them to the side.

So I went to buy the jeans and decided to keep that perfume hidden. It was a seven-dollar bottle, for gosh sakes! But I thought I was above the law, and tried to steal it. When I was leaving, every security person in the store swarmed me like it was a scene out of *Cops*. They had three squad cars outside for one small bottle of perfume. I'd never gotten in trouble with the law before, so I was completely embarrassed.

"I swear, I forgot that bottle was even in the pocket!" I screamed to the security guards. I was totally lying through my teeth because I was terrified.

When I got to court, the judge looked me in the eye and asked, "How do you plead?"

Just then, I heard the other side.

"Tell the truth, and that will help you. You will learn from this."

I looked at the judge and told him what really happened.

"I did take the perfume, Your Honor. I'm sorry," I said.

He shot me a very disappointed look and threw the book at me.

"I could make your fine be anything between a hundred and five hundred dollars, and I'm making yours five hundred," he said.

At that time, five hundred dollars felt like a million. I heard the other side as I soaked in my punishment.

"Are you going to learn from this, or do this again?"

We go through life like we are walking across a pond, and there are these stepping stones that we see as we approach, and we have to choose which stone to step on. I made a wrong step by stealing that perfume. And I got soaking wet. By accepting the responsibility and the consequences that went with it, I knew I never would take anything that didn't belong to me again.

If I could take back that day I bailed on Mark and go to that wedding, I would. Even though I didn't feel about him the way he felt about me, I should have kept my end of the bargain. Will I ever really feel good about the way I behaved? No. But I've had to learn to say to myself, "You've gotta let this go, because it's a part of being human." If I could take back the day I stole the perfume,

I'd certainly pay more attention to the very clear message I was hearing from the other side and I wouldn't have tried to swipe it. I knew it was wrong all along. But, here on this side of the veil, there is no such thing as perfection, and some things we just have to learn the hard way.

A middle-aged man came to see me for a reading, but he also had something he wanted to get off his chest. He told me he hadn't been living in a way he was proud of. He knew he hadn't been a good husband; he'd cheated on his wife. She hadn't found out, but he carried the guilt. He also knew he hadn't been a good father. He loved his kids, he told me, and he made sure that they had whatever they needed in a material sense, but he had not given them his time. He wasn't around for them.

He'd had a heart attack and was having surgery to have a stent put in. During surgery, he had a near-death episode. He felt like he was out of his body and traveled to the other side. There, he said, he spoke with someone whom he recognized, but it wasn't someone he knew in this life, it was someone he believed he knew from a past life. He told this person all his concerns and regrets and had the clear understanding that he was being given another chance to do better. When he came back into his body, he was determined to do just that.

He said, "I know this sounds crazy."

I said, "Nope. It never sounds crazy to me, honey. Remember who you are talking to!"

We shared a laugh. Then he said he was doing the best he could to change his ways and live a better life. He hasn't cheated again; he's doing his best to spend time with his kids, from soccer games to homework, all kinds of things he said he had never done before, things he'd put on his wife as if it were all her job. He said he wasn't angry anymore; he was calmer and more forgiving. But what made him feel the most changed is that he laughed more. He said he used to be always in a sulky mood, never saw the humor in things, and got annoyed when people around him seemed to laugh easily. "Now," he said, "I laugh every chance I get, and I just feel better for it."

Here's an interesting thing. On the other side of the veil is complete peace and harmony. We do have a life review when we cross, and we come to see the harm we have done as well as the good things we've done. Then *all is forgiven*. But the spirits still are so grateful if they get a chance to apologize for anything they feel they messed up, and will take any opportunity they can find to comfort a loved one here, especially if they believe they have wronged that person in some way when they were in the flesh.

At a recent show in Fairfield, New Jersey, I called on a young man who was hoping to speak to his mom. She came through quickly and said that he looked just like her. Actually, she said that if we put a wig on him, he would look just like her, which made me smile. He was the apple of her eye. And he confirmed that he did indeed resemble his mother. But more importantly, his biological father came through. His dad apologized to him for not being there for him in his life. This meant a lot to him because he'd never had a good relationship with his dad, and he always wanted an apology when his father was alive but had never gotten one. Clearly, once over there, his dad realized that his behavior toward his son had hurt him, and he grabbed the chance to try to make amends.

Nearly every single one of us has done things in our lives that we are not proud of. I remember a client I read for whose mother came through and mentioned a car accident, saying to him, "It's not your fault." She went on to say that, on the other side, unconditional love was waiting for him. I had no idea why she felt he needed that message, but he got very emotional and confessed to me that he felt horribly guilt-ridden and filled with sadness because he had been in a car accident and the person he was with in the car, the driver, was unconscious. He left the scene of the accident, left this person unconscious. He was involved with this person in some way that he did not want his wife or family to know about. I'm not sure exactly what the story was, maybe an affair or maybe just someone his family felt very strongly about, to the point where he'd promised not to see them. The driver of the vehicle did not die, but he felt like a coward for leaving the scene when they were helpless, and he was unable to forgive himself. It happened long ago. The other person recovered and had a life, but because he had not stuck around, he carried this guilt all these years and wondered what his judgment would be on the other side. Of course the accident wasn't his fault, as he wasn't driving. But his concern was about leaving. However, his mother kept repeating that he would be met by unconditional love. She said to him, "Don't ever be afraid of God," and that he would not be judged. I hoped hearing this from her would reassure him that God is great and God is good.

I've given this a lot of thought over the years, both because of my own human experiences and because of the stories my clients tell me. I know that guilt must serve some positive purpose or it would never exist. The guilt that I feel, I choose to feel over and over for some reason. It can of course help me remember to treat others the way I'd like to be treated while I'm still alive.

But I don't have to keep judging myself so harshly for the rest of my life. On the other side, you don't have to relive these difficult moments over and over. Apparently, in our life review, we witness it only once, and we quickly get the perspective of the ones we hurt.

So, in my life review, I will experience a moment where I'll be in Mark's shoes, and I will feel all the pain and rejection that he experienced because of my behavior—with the full understanding that *I* caused that pain.

Ouch!

But, along with these really unpleasant episodes (and others—we all have them), I will also feel all the love I gave to my parents, my brother, my husband, my entire family, and all my dear friends. Every heartfelt moment, and every pissed-off moment. It all comes flooding back in an instant.

Believe it or not, we watch this life review without judgment. It just *happens*, kind of like when you watch a sporting event you don't really care for, like maybe a soccer match when you don't understand the game all that well. You're just observing these people as they run around in circles in these silly-looking shorts on the soccer field, and you really don't give a damn who just scored. (Any soccer fans, please forgive me. I just don't get this game.) It's not *bad* and it's not *good*. It just *is*. That is how the dead folks explain the life review. They watch and acknowledge it, but they don't judge it. It's about *understanding*, not punishment. And in my work, I've seen a lot of healing happen after the dead see their life review. People who treated others very badly "get it" and they want to make amends.

One example of this came from a woman whose husband had passed. After I'd delivered a number of messages that validated for her that this was indeed her husband, he mentioned something he had written. This was an unusual case because, usually, when a spirit refers to something they have written, they seem very happy about it, but in this case I could tell he had a lot of remorse surrounding it. Then he said, "I'm sorry for the list. I'm sorry, forgive me." I had no idea what he was referring to, but the woman told me that after her husband died, she'd found a list of complaints he'd written out, about his life, his wife, and his family! Needless to say, discovering this had broken her heart, and as she told the story, she was crying. Then he said, "Please remember Paris." My client looked up—she had also found a postcard from when they were first married. He'd gone to Paris for work and he'd written her a postcard where he'd professed his love for her and wrote about their dreams for their life together. He had put a heart symbol on the card, which he showed me. As I conveyed this to her, she smiled.

All of us do things we regret. We all would like to have some kind of do-over for things we've said or done.

Here among the living, even when we say we forgive someone, do we really do it? Think about this for a second. In our world, if you get in a fight with someone, or if someone has an affair with your husband, and then they come up to you and they're big enough to say, "I'm truly sorry about that. Do you forgive me?"

You might say, "Sure, I forgive you." But it's very hard. Again, we are human, not perfect. We are emotional. And the reality is, we probably store that memory away. We forgive *part* of it, but we're still holding on to those feelings of disappointment and betrayal. We're still keeping score. We might be out laughing and talking to them and having a good time, but in the back of our minds, we're still thinking, *I remember what you did, you jerk!*

I've had clients ask me about the role karma plays in all our "crimes and misdemeanors." Karma is nearly always a part of it, and certainly any such action will accrue karma that we'll have to offset, either in this lifetime or in one to come. There's also such a thing as instant karma, when we zing someone, whether intentionally or not, and we get zinged right back almost immediately. There's also such a thing as literally attracting powerful negative energy by our behavior and losing control of our emotions.

Early in life, we choose our moral compass, but temptation is continually put before us; opportunities to behave thoughtlessly don't magically end once we're no longer children. There are lessons, lessons, and more lessons (though we *do* usually get to have some fun in there too!). The karma we bring with us from past lives guarantees we'll have things we need to work through with specific people or situations. And we all have a mix of character traits, some positive and some that need polishing. One of mine is impatience with idiots. Oh, I would love to be that person who handles every stressful situation with good grace. But I still, unfortunately, have a long way to go—and believe me, Satan knows this!

I recall a situation, not that long ago, when I was driving to get a manicure and pedicure. My best friend Mushy, who has been my sidekick my whole life, moved to Florida. I really missed her, and she was in town for a visit and I was going out to dinner with her and the rest of the Jersey girls in our gang. Nails all done, I was driving home to change, and running pretty late, so I was already anxious. I was on a twisty thirty-five-mile-per-hour country road when some *mamaluke* (For those of you who are not Italian, "mamaluke" basically means "idiot.") pulled out in front of me and then proceeded to go *ten* miles an hour. Already, I was nuts, and she kept stepping on her brakes—on, off, on, off—making me completely crazy. Finally I got to a place where I could pass her, and I grabbed the opportunity. But as I passed her, she had her window down and was screaming at me! Screaming at *me???* Are you *kidding* me? She was the one driving like she'd never seen a car before, and she was screaming at me? How dare she! Well, I then returned the favor. I was yelling and waving, and I could literally feel the devil right beside me, happy about the whole thing. My body was literally shaking. I got home and jumped in the shower, still really angry. As I was washing my hair, I looked down and noticed that the water was not going down the drain; it was pooling and getting deeper, and then flooding over the edge of the shower onto the bathroom floor. I started freaking out. I had to run and grab towels to mop up all the water. As I was doing this, I yelled to John. He was going out, too, so I told him to use the other shower because the drain was clogged in this one. I had no idea what was causing it. We've had problems with drains backing up when water froze in the pipes, but it was summer, so that didn't make any sense. Of course, that night when we were both home, John told me that he'd used the same shower I had with no problem at all. No clog, no water backing up. And since then, it has never done it again. What happened?

Okay, here's what I believe. When I became irritated with the other driver, I let down my guard. I was already in an anxious state, not thinking properly, and allowing my emotions to run wild. (In hindsight, how terrible would it have been if I had been fifteen minutes late to see my girlfriends?) That allowed negative energy to get right next to me, and it hung on and stayed there.

I did not have the presence of mind to ask God or the spirits for help. If there was a better angel on my shoulder, suggesting that I take a chill pill, I was so irritated I couldn't hear it. I "handled the situation" myself, by acting like a maniac. I practically invited the evil energy to cling to me with all my screaming, and it literally followed me home.

It was my choice.

After I had this realization, I was able to breathe deeply, calm myself, and then pray. First I prayed for God's help, demanding in the name of God that the negativity, the devil, if you will, leave me. Then I prayed for forgiveness and for peace.

We all have our own challenges, we all make mistakes. But we can all get help and choose to make a change. It's our decision!

On the other side, yes, the spirits see everything we do. They know everything. But it's not like Santa Claus, seeing everything and making a list. They also see our heart. And there is no judgment, it's *gone*. The forgiveness is real. The "I remember what you did" is not there anymore. There's no filing cabinet. Just like that journalist's grandfather and father standing arm in arm: All is forgiven.

Only love matters.

So that's the difference. When a spirit says, *"It's okay. Let it go. We forgive you,"* they mean it. It's forgotten.

If we really do feel rotten about something we've done, we can use it as an opportunity to learn and grow spiritually. Sometimes it's important to hold onto the feeling we've done something wrong for a while—it can be a vivid reminder that we don't want to behave like that again. But once we've gotten the lesson down, it's not necessary to carry around the guilt anymore. We can forgive ourselves. We'll still see it in our life review on the other side, but some of the sting might be taken away if we know it's something we've healed while we are here, rather than something we did nothing to correct and carried around all our lives.

So, as you doze off to sleep, try practicing forgiveness, both for others who might have treated you thoughtlessly or unkindly, and for yourself if you haven't quite lived up to your own ideals in some of your behavior. Practice real and authentic forgiveness, not the kind that is convenient, but the kind that surrounds you like a cape and hugs you.

I forgive. I choose love. We are all one.

Chapter 5

Let Your Freak Flag Fly (You Be You)

While we are here on Planet Earth, each of us has a divine purpose. This might be a particular talent, something that we discover we are better at than others are, something we are passionate about, and that gives our life its shape or meaning. Or it might be something—some mission—that we find ourselves uniquely placed to take on or do. God has given each of us this "something special." It's what makes us who we are and colors how we think and what we do. Our divine purpose allows us to be some kind of force in the world. I have always had a gift for entertaining, and I know that I have been one kind of entertainer or another in multiple lifetimes. But I'm not Meryl Streep. She is brilliantly gifted in the way she can *become* a character and tell a story. What gives my ability to entertain its divine purpose is that added something—my ability to connect with the other side. It allows me to bring messages to folks here, and in that way, I'm able to give a lot of reassurance and comfort.

Sometimes what we are here to do is a total mystery to us. This can be incredibly frustrating! But do not lose heart. Each and every one of us has a divine purpose. Anyone who is looking for their own divine purpose may have to be willing to think deeply about what matters to them and sift through multiple layers of clues. For example, as I've said, I love performing. But my purpose goes at least one layer beyond that to my other ability. The two come together to allow me to make a difference in the world. Somebody else might be very good at numbers—does that mean they are meant to be a mathematician? Not necessarily. Maybe they also love animals, and their skill with numbers will allow them to keep the books for an organization that cares for wildlife. Another person may have a gift for imparting learning. Will they be a teacher? Not necessarily. Maybe they will simply be a mentor, or maybe it is their true divine purpose to be a

parent who will use all their talents of communication and
creativity and patience to raise great kids. Maybe you already had
an entire career. You went to school, took something sensible
that made your parents happy, got a good job, and worked your
way to retirement. And not until now have you had a chance to
take a breath and really think about where your true passions
lie. Will you begin to paint and discover a new world of colorful
creativity, bringing joy to others? Will you recognize that your
true divine purpose is your lifelong desire to teach and mentor
a young person just embarking on the career you have already
finished? Jimmy Carter had a career as a farmer; I imagine
he was good at that. Then he was the president of the United
States—that's a pretty big deal. But when he left office, he built
houses with Habitat for Humanity. That was his passion: to
help others.

Or look at José Andrés. He is a Michelin-starred chef. Cooking
is in his blood, and yes, in his very soul. Very few restaurateurs
ever achieve this level of recognition. But when Hurricane Maria
left millions of people in Puerto Rico without power and food, he
left his restaurant and went there to set up giant food kitchens,
serving thousands. Clearly, this was his divine mission.

I'm a huge fan of Bette Midler. She's a fabulous singer and
performer. But I really admire her passion for giving back to her
home city of New York and the planet in general, wanting to have
it clean and beautiful. She helps clean up neighborhoods that
have been trashed and creates gardens. That's a divine purpose
in my book; this passion for making things beautiful comes from
her very soul.

In my own circle, my dear friend Ginger Grancognolo is most
certainly living her divine purpose. When she was a young girl,

she had some truly terrible experiences and suffered unspeakable trauma. I don't say this in judgment, but a lot of people who have had such experiences will find pretty negative ways to cope, including excessive drinking or drug use, or at the very least become sad, depressed, or negative people. This girl has not only risen above this, she has trained herself, educated herself, and become a shining example of what you can be when you choose wisely. She has absolutely become her most divine self and went on to give back to the world. She is the most unselfish person I have ever met. She teaches, she sees clients, she gives her personal time to others. She has helped people to recover from all sorts of things that have happened to them in their lives. She works with severely depressed people and children who are struggling with issues of abuse or abandonment. For me personally, she has shown me a road and taught me how to use it, my path back to God. Given where I am now, this may seem strange, but before I worked with Ginger, I didn't even know how to talk to God. When I went into a house of worship of any kind, I didn't feel worthy. I felt uncomfortable. She's the one who taught me that I was worthy, that anyone can talk to God. No special language is necessary; it comes from your heart and through your soul. Through her teaching, I gained a window to communicate with the other side in a way I never had before. I'm grateful that she was living her divine purpose, because it helped me be able to live mine!

We're here for such a relatively short time, so it's important for us to be our true, best selves. This is how we are happy and how we can help make others happy, too.

Everyone is beautiful in her or his own way. And yet, we live in a world of judgment. Whether we admit it or not, we all make judgments, and we all are judged by others. It's a constant process of evaluation, every single day. What we need to work on is managing both sides of this. First, to be sure that the judgments we are making about others are not ones that look to tear somebody down to make ourselves feel superior, like body-shaming or talking about someone who maybe doesn't have the wherewithal to dress in the latest fashions or just has a different cultural or personal style (I don't want to see stories about young girls being sent home from school for wearing their hair in braids!). I saw on Twitter a while back how kids at school were bullying a young boy because he liked to wear nail polish—the color he was wearing was one he said he thought was cool, and it was one of the colors of his favorite sports team. I was so happy to see that his dad stuck up for him, as did many other people responding to the post. In a follow-up, the boy thanked everyone for taking his side and supporting him. I really hope that we all will be seeing more of this—support for our differences, rather than trying to drag down someone with their own unique charm and trying to make them feel bad about themselves. It's easy enough to say, "Well it's not *my* taste, but you do you!"

In making judgments—which are simply part of the way our human brains work—we can look at others to see what qualities we *admire* and might like to try to develop in ourselves. Maybe we'd like to be as brave as that boy, rocking his nail polish just because he liked it. Maybe we'd like to be as protective and supportive as those who wrote and said, "Do your thing, kiddo—I've got your back!" Sometimes, when we stick up for the underdog, we put ourselves out on a limb. It can feel lonely and scary out there, even if, in our heart of hearts, we know it's the right thing to do (the thing we *want* to do) because it makes us the person we want to be, a person worth admiring. We need to bear in mind that, even if it seems like we're all alone, the spirits who care about us are there too. You can always talk to them and ask them to help you feel courageous, or to aid your efforts if there's some action you need to take in order to see justice done or maintained.

At the same time, we need to guard ourselves to not take others' opinions about us—what we look like, how we dress, what we want to do with our lives, and so forth—so seriously that they make us feel bad about ourselves. Sometimes even *we* don't know the path we are on until things become clearer, so needless to say, others are not qualified to critique. Just take any comments with a grain of salt—or a ladle of marinara sauce if you're Italian! I know this can be really hard, especially for younger people or sensitive types who don't have a very thick skin. And with all the crazy stuff that social media has brought us, like online bullying, other people's opinions of us can be hard to avoid and can work their way under our skin.

I mentioned in an earlier book that my niece, Bobbie Concetta, has some psychic ability. This seems to be particularly in regard to pets and other animals. She's so in tune that she can tell when they are not well. There was a cat that looked fine to me, but Bobbie Concetta knew there was something very wrong and was concerned. Sure enough, when she took the cat to the vet, it could not be saved.

By the time this book comes out, Bobbie Concetta will be eighteen. We don't yet know what her divine purpose may turn out to be. It may be using her ability or it may be something else, but knowing some of the misunderstanding and mean comments I had to weather when I came out with my own ability (and I heard stories from my father about challenges my grandfather experienced; I even had to convince my own skeptical husband before he became one of my greatest champions), I do worry a little bit for her. There are a lot of people who just like to torment anyone they see as "different." She's such a sweet, kind soul, without one mean bone in her entire body. It worries me that she is too defenseless. I want her to be free to be who she is and fulfill her purpose here. I'll be keeping an eye on her, and I know her angels and protectors on the other side will be, too.

My brother Harold and I were what they call "Irish twins," meaning that we were born less than a year apart. As brother and sister, we were extremely close. When I was sixteen, a guy I knew at school said to me, "You know, your brother is a faggot."

At the time, I had no idea that my brother was gay. I got very upset and angry and said, "That's not true!" But when I was seventeen, my brother told me himself that he was gay. This was like the Dark Ages; there was so little understanding or acceptance of being gay at that time. I confess that I was very disappointed. I thought only of myself: How would I explain this to the Italian stallions I was dating? I was angry because I thought he would never marry or have children, never giving a thought to what he needed or what he was going through. I'm really ashamed to say this, and it breaks my heart, looking back, that this was my first reaction.

Harold came out when he was just eighteen years old. Today that might not seem so incredible, but back when we were teens, announcing you were gay was way scarier. All too frequently, coming out of the proverbial closet meant putting yourself on the front line for every kind of abuse and mistreatment. Harold would not live a lie, but still, he cried when he told my parents, worried that this was something a six-foot-two Sicilian man (our father) would be ashamed of. Instead, my dad told him, "You are my son. I don't care what you are, I love you and I'm proud of you. Furthermore, if anyone has a problem with that, they have to go through me first!" And today I am infinitely proud of my father who was certainly ahead of his time with his stance of acceptance, understanding, and love.

What my father knew is that "straight or gay" does not define the person. My brother had way more to him. He was the very definition of kindness and generosity. He would give anyone the shirt off his back, and he always looked out for and doted on me. When I was thirteen, all the girls in my school had "falls"— these were hairpieces made out of human hair! They went for eighty dollars. I assure you that at age thirteen I did not have eighty dollars, and unfortunately my parents declined to buy me this "must-have" item. Harold was just fourteen but worked part-time at the Pine Brook Auction Market in Pine Brook, New Jersey. (This was a big landmark in the 1960s, but burned down sometime in the early 1980s.) Eighty dollars was a huge sum to him, too, but Harold could not be underestimated. My sweet brother worked all summer saving that money. He bought me the fall, and I was beyond thrilled. But he was like this with everyone. He loved to cook big elaborate dinners with all the trimmings; he took care of everyone. That's what gave him pleasure.

My parents were of different religions and ethnicities (Irish and Italian, two that never mixed back in the day); my older brother was gay. My younger brother married a Chinese-American woman, adding yet another ethnicity to our nicely mixed family. I believe that having so many different colors on my family palette, so to speak, allows me to relate to virtually anyone I encounter without judgment, only love. I'm still human, I am not perfect, and I sometimes have to wrestle with my fears. But I understand what the goal is and why it is worth it.

I was walking through the town of Boonton, where I live, and I ran into the mayor. He knows me, and he greeted me as he was walking down the street with his husband. We chatted for a bit, and he told me that he was trying very hard to learn the craft of mediumship. I offered him a few tips and then said, "Here, I'll show you." His husband was standing next to him, and I asked him to say his name, which he did. I said, "Okay, this is what I have: something about California that's calling you; either you want to go there, or there's something significant there for you. There's something about your father who passed away, who very much wants to apologize to you." His father was explaining that he missed the chance to tell his son how proud he was of him in this life, and that he was not upset with his lifestyle. He described a number of different articles of clothing that his son would recognize and mentioned a few things only his son would understand—one had to do with hiking when he and his siblings were young kids. The father mentioned a special moment they had shared, something to do with a man-to-man understanding of fishing—apparently fishing was something they had enjoyed doing together. He was verifying all these things, and by this time the mayor's husband was in tears.

The messages were very simple, but the mayor said to me, "Concetta, you have no idea what you just did. You have no idea how much he needed to hear this and what you said and how much sense it made." I told him it's always the individual on the other side that I count on to bring the message, because I myself don't know what I'm talking about!

They both said, "I'm sure it wasn't a coincidence we ran into you on the street today." It was clear that the messages I was able to share brought healing, which I feel is a profound honor and gift— an example of my own divine purpose.

I had a client in my office who also brought this home to me. After her reading, she said, "What makes your work so beautiful, Concetta, is that every one of us has a fear of dying, and what awaits all of us. And you do help take that fear away."

I said, "Honey, I may not be perfect or have all the answers, but there's one thing I can tell you: In all my life hearing dead folks, and in my entire career doing readings for people, I've never heard anyone complain about the other side. All they ever talk about is what a miracle it is. I'm just like anyone else, and I too have just a smidgen of fear, like any human would have, of the unknown. But I do know that God is good, and so his realm has to be good. And that gives me a lot of comfort."

Not everyone will have an easy time becoming who and what they are meant to be. Sometimes it takes many years even to discover what we are intended for. And it can take a lot of hard work and real courage—whether it's because others feel threatened by your uniqueness, or whether you just feel unsupported in your dreams. My brother Harold was always a fan of Jimi Hendrix, and when I hear Jimi's music, I always think of him. There are a couple of lines in Jimi's song "If Six Was Nine" that I bet he really related to—when Jimi sings, "I've got my own world to live through...and I ain't gonna copy you...I'm gonna wave my freak flag high!" he's saying everyone has to be *who* they are, *what* they are, not what somebody else would prefer they be.

As challenging as that may be here (and I know it can be very hard), you have to understand that there are those on the other side who are really your guardian angels—we all have them, not just a select lucky few. And those spirits will be very much looking out for you and supporting you in any way they possibly can.

A while back, a young man came to me. He was very good-looking, gorgeous and blonde. He was German, and he told me he still had family back in Germany. His family here was very much against gay people, and he himself was gay. I can tell you that there was nothing in his demeanor that would have suggested to me this truth, certainly nothing of any stereotype some people have about how a gay person looks, sounds, or behaves. But it was a big fear of his that his family would discover his secret and he'd be ostracized. In the reading, his grandfather came through to tell him that there was more love for him within the family than he knew. His grandfather told him that *he* loved him—always had and always would—and that he would show him signs that he did. He also told this young man that he should be who he was and not to be afraid to live his life honestly.

Some time after his reading, a family member who was still in Germany passed away. I assume it was when the family was going through this person's things that they'd found a photograph, one they sent to him. It was a photo of his grandfather holding him when he was a baby. And great love was obvious in the grandfather's eyes. He took that as a major sign—he'd never even known the photo existed.

When you hold back from being your authentic self, you are not being true to your soul's path. Nobody can be their best self if they are trying to conform to be like everybody else. We each have our own divine purpose here. It's *our* purpose, not somebody else's.

I have a friend who lives in New York City. One of her favorite things is people-watching. She's said that, if you live in New York long enough, you start to think that nothing can surprise you—until it does. Every time you think you've seen the craziest thing you could ever see, somebody tops it. (I'm not talking about "crazy dangerous" or "crazy hurtful." I mean like some sort of costume, invention, display, or performance.) Where she lives, it's common to see people sharing their gifts, whether it's an opera singer or guitarist or drummer on a subway platform, or someone dancing with a life-size puppet in Times Square. I remember one time she told me about being in Central Park and seeing a guy wearing a swallowtail tuxedo jacket riding one of those old-fashioned bicycles with the great big wheel in the front (I don't know how they even get up on one of those things). And as she watched him, just loving the novelty of seeing such a thing, she saw behind him there were *a dozen more* people riding these bikes through the park in a wave! Think what that does to an ordinary day to see something so fun and unexpected. You can't help but smile. You might look at this as "crazy," but I say, "Let your freak flag fly!" Life would be so dull without different people doing different things, things we might never have thought of. My friend is a businessperson and tends to dress in a fairly mainstream way, but because she gets such a kick out of seeing all the weird and wonderful folks around her, every now and then she'll dress up in something just a little bit different, to "give back" some enjoyment to other people-watchers for all the fun she's had watching.

We are all one, but we are each unique. We each have a special reason for being here—each of us has our *own* reality show, and we need to own our starring role in it. The other side wants us to respect and appreciate each other, help and support each other whenever we can, and allow each other to be who they are meant to be here on Planet Earth.

In case this has all sounded a little too serious, it's perfectly okay to have a little fun. I'm thinking back to this past Halloween— John and I were invited to a party with a bunch of friends, and he didn't have a costume. I had mine all ready, and I said, "John, what are you going to do?"

He said, "I don't know. I was thinking of going as a cowboy."

I said, "A cowboy?" With a cowboy costume you have to have things like a cowboy hat, a gun, a holster. That was out of the question—we didn't have any of those things. So I said, "Why don't you go as something completely opposite of what you are?"

He said, "What's that?" I said, "A woman."

Well, to be honest, I was saying it for fun, but he cracked up and said, "What would I wear?" So I started pulling together some of my clothes—he's thin and has a great body, so he was able to fit into my things. As I was getting him a dress, a shawl, a bracelet, and a ring, he said he wanted to do the shoes too. I had a pair of bright red ones he managed to squeeze into. Then he said he wanted a matching pocketbook.

I had just bought a really pretty red pocketbook and I said, "Oh no you don't, you are *not* wearing my brand new pocketbook!" We were just cracking up the whole time we were putting this together. But then, when I was putting lipstick on John, it went from "funny" to…I don't know. I was used to my husband being the suave, dapper "Johnny Fontaine." John has always been an impeccable dresser, and I've always been a sucker for that Italian stallion who dresses well. So to see him driving to this party wearing red lipstick, a dress, a shawl, earrings, and necklace to match—I just couldn't stop laughing. But at one point I said to him, "Are you comfortable with this?"

He said, "I don't care!" He was just having fun. My husband is so comfortable in his own skin that I have to say that's one of the things that turns me on about him. The party was great, and John's outfit was a big hit. The next day, we were going to the mall, and he got all dressed up in full Guido, like he was going to a mob meeting. The "other" John was back in the closet.

This is your reality show. *Your* reality. *Your* show. Every day, you need to put aside any negative judgments of others, as well as others' judgments about you. Look to the positive—what are you really here for? Who do you want to be? What have you come to contribute or accomplish? Who are the right role models for you? We need to ask the other side to help clear the path for the special work we are here to do; we need to pray, saying, "I am calm, important, loved, healthy, happy, and most importantly, grounded in God." Then let your freak flag fly and get on with what you have come here to do!

Chapter 6

One Pill Makes You Larger…and One Pill Makes You Small

I remember a show I was doing in Totowa, New Jersey. A woman's deceased brother came through, appearing to me in a haze of smoke. Often I will smell cigarette smoke or pipe tobacco—the perception will be pretty specific. I said to the woman, "There's all this smoke around him—and it's not *all* cigarette smoke."

She laughed out loud and then said, "Well, he did go to Woodstock!"

You can't turn on the TV now without seeing a story about drugs. This is something that until recent generations had never been much of a "thing" for most people, throughout many reincarnations. Yes, we've long had people who have struggled with alcoholism and have heard stories of "opium dens" from the time of the British East India Company. I don't recall myself having a past life that involved anything like that. But, more recently, drugs have touched or taken over so many lives. Besides all the medications available now, whether over-the-counter or prescribed, there are the less legal kinds—some taken because of an addiction and some for "entertainment." This isn't a subject I might raise here, except that more and more I'm seeing folks who have lost a loved one to an overdose. Needless to say, this causes tremendous pain, so it's obviously one of our lessons here on the earth plane. There's been a lot of movement toward legalizing marijuana for its therapeutic uses, and I recently read how even certain other drugs that had been outlawed, when they were misused for partying, are now being studied to see if they can help people with addictions and anxiety. I'll leave that to the scientists to figure out, but I will tell my own story as a cautionary tale!

One of the things that I *know* as a medium is that people who have heightened sensitivities (either with intuition or the ability to see spirits of the deceased) should NOT do drugs. I, unfortunately, had to learn this lesson the hard way, because when peer pressure kicked in during high school, I found myself dabbling in some things I probably shouldn't have.

When I was sixteen, my best friend Mushy and I decided to go against our better judgment and take LSD. The place: a double feature at the movies. Other classmates had occasionally smoked pot, but every time it was passed to me, I would fake it and never inhale. I just had a feeling it wouldn't agree with me. Why I thought jumping from doing nothing to trying "purple haze" was a good idea, I'll never know, but I digress.

The first movie they were playing was called *Charly*, which was about a mentally challenged guy who takes a drug that makes him go from being not too sharp, to someone who is super smart. But the drug doesn't last, so at the end of the movie, he goes back to being mentally challenged.

Holy moly!

The second movie was called *They Shoot Horses, Don't They?* with Jane Fonda, about a couple struggling though a dance marathon. Couples basically keep going until they can't move anymore and just drop from exhaustion, trying to win a money prize. The premise of that movie is that they shoot the horses when they no longer have value. Also, Jane Fonda's character wanted the guy in the movie (Michael Sarrazin) to shoot her.

Both of these movies were not only depressing, but confusing as hell when you're under the influence of LSD.

It took a little while for the drug to hit me, but when it hit—*holy crap*, did it hit. Colors were brighter. The walls were moving. My hearing got so sensitive I thought I could actually hear people in the lobby from my seat in the theater. I was begging Mushy to hold my hand because I couldn't handle it. I definitely didn't see how anyone could do this for fun! Even the sounds of the man chewing popcorn behind me were making me nuts. Each bite sounded like a bomb going off, and I swear I could hear his tongue hit the roof of his mouth.

Then I started hearing people talking to me, only I didn't know if that was my mind or the dead folks.

Is that a spirit or am I tripping?!

I couldn't make out who was real and who wasn't. As I looked over my shoulder to the left of the loud popcorn dude, there were people sitting there laughing at me and talking to me...only they were freaking dead!!

"Mushy, do you see those dead people?" I whispered.

"Concetta, you're freaking me out!" she said.

There was a break between the movies so people could stretch their legs or go to the bathroom. I dragged Mushy out to the lobby with me to escape the terrifying sounds of that man's exploding popcorn kernels and the yapping dead guys. To get there, we had to go up this spiral staircase. With each step, I thought I was going to lose my balance, fall down, and crack my head open. Each step I took felt like an earthquake was hitting New Jersey.

Boom! Boom!

We finally made it to the top of the stairs and got to the bathroom. As we walked in, I was just glued to the wall, hoping it would make me feel grounded or something, because I was feeling so out of my mind. Everything looked like it was in Technicolor, but on steroids, so the reds were *really* red, and the blues were this incredible blue hue I'd never seen before. I was scanning the room and I saw this woman putting on lipstick, and her lips looked like they were stretching out like chewing gum. I was watching her so intently with my eyes bugging out, I'm surprised she didn't call the cops—I must have looked so insane. Then I heard whispers...and I knew it was the dead trying to get my attention: "Sorry, folks, this medium is currently *out of order!*"

When Mushy came out of the stall, I pointed to the woman's lips and said, "Do you see that, Mushy?" because her lips looked like they were being stretched to Texas. But Mushy was having a perfectly fine trip and kept trying to get me under control. She wasn't seeing stretched-out lips. She wanted to get back to the movie. Now, I'll talk to spirits all day long (unless I'm on LSD, that is!), but watching someone's lips melt, now *that* stuff is scary!

We left the bathroom, headed down the spiral staircase of doom, and made it back into the theater just in time for *They Shoot Horses, Don't They?* Again, I was begging Mushy to hold my hand because, at this point, I'm thinking the chair is trying to swallow me.

You'll be fine, Concetta. Try to relax.

My father was picking us up after the movie, and I was terrified he might figure out that we had taken something and were tripping. When we walked out of the theater to cross the street, I felt like Wendy in *Peter Pan*, walking the plank—that walk seemed to take *forever*. Looking at all the other people leaving the theater, I was convinced they were talking about me. That's another thing that happens to sensitive people under the influence...we think *everyone* is talking about us and become extremely paranoid.

When I got home and went to my room, I heard my parents whispering in the living room. I thought I heard my mother saying to my father, "I think Connie is high on LSD!"

And what I thought I heard my father say in return was, "Yeah, I could tell!"

The next thing I knew, I was storming into the living room yelling, "I'm not taking drugs! I am *not* on LSD!" And my mother's head slowly did this 180-degree turn like an owl, where her body didn't budge.

She looked at me and said in a calm tone, "We weren't talking about you, Con."

"Oh, okay," I said, and I made my way down to my brother Harold's room. He was sleeping, but I woke him up.

"Harold," I whispered. "I'm on LSD. What do I do?"

He smiled and said, "Hey, cool, enjoy it!"

I wasn't enjoying *anything*. The LSD didn't wear off until lunch *the next day*. I could barely make it through math class because

I could see my teacher surrounded by all the spirits of her deceased family! Being in this post-LSD fog meant I couldn't control my abilities. I was sensitive to begin with, but the chemicals of the drug took me to a place I never wanted to return to. I knew, from that moment on, I could never do drugs again— one more lesson learned on the earth plane!

For me to be in any kind of jeopardized consciousness, whether it's with alcohol or drugs, is not a good thing. I may joke about having cocktails, but the truth is that I don't drink; I don't like anything that hinders my conscious mind. Mushy could quickly bounce back and recover because she doesn't have the spiritual connection that I have. But for anyone with a heightened sense of intuition, taking something that alters your senses—either drugs or alcohol, or even anesthesia—can really screw with your abilities. If I'm telling the whole truth, then I have to say that trip with Mushy wasn't the last time that I tried drugs. Teenagers are more stupid than other people. There were times when I wanted to be "cool" or be in with the "in crowd," so I made some other mistakes, but none as severe as the one I made when I took that acid trip, thank God. Of course, after our wild night, Mushy used to tease me. She'd say, "Don't let Connie in a room where they even smoked pot ten days ago, 'cause she'll get high just inhaling the residue."

There are some sensitive people who actually try to dull their abilities by partying. They hope this will turn it off, even just for a moment. I understand this inclination, because if you haven't learned how to control the on/off switch, it can be quite stressful to be so sensitive or have the dead intruding on you day and night. I see this a lot in my industry. But the danger is that this can actually open you up to dark energies.

During one of my live events, I remember a woman who wanted to connect to her son. As soon as she said his name, he came right through, standing by his mother.

"I see him," I said. "He's wearing a leather jacket."

"Yes, he always wore a leather jacket," she said with a cracked half-smile. This woman was still grieving and clutched a tissue to wipe her eyes. Then the son showed me how he died. He apparently took too many pills of some kind and accidentally killed himself. He was addicted to the pills and thought he was just going to get high, but unfortunately he ended his life.

"He's taking responsibility for his actions," I said. "He knows he made a terrible mistake. But he just couldn't kick it. He had a lot of bad people around him and he just couldn't get it together."

The woman let out a heavy sob.

Apparently the young man had a lot of anxiety, and he took an anti-anxiety drug to calm his nerves. Eventually he got addicted, and his addiction moved to opioids. This is a slippery slope that I see all the time. People are anxious, or they may have physical pain, and they're getting hooked on pills, and now we have an opioid epidemic on our hands.

"He doesn't want you to blame yourself," I said. "He really wants you to know that you did the best you could. You were a fantastic mom."

"We tried to get him into rehab," the woman said. "He never stayed. We tried tough love, and then tried letting him live with us. But after a while, we couldn't live with him anymore, because we were always fighting."

Often, addicts will have spirits (who were looking for a place to camp out) attached to their energy fields.. These souls aren't in the light, and they want to stay that way. Their dark energies can cause people who live in the house to have arguments. These spirits like to have company, so they try to bring you down to their energetic level.

Her son showed me how he flicks the light switches on and off in the house to let her know he is around.

"He messes with the lights," I said. "He wants you to know that when you see the lights flicker, it is him."

The mother laughed.

"Yeah, that happens a lot," she said.

"But just know he has a clear mind now," I said. "He sees how much this has hurt you and he is so sorry. He wants you to know that he is happy and can help from the other side with his brother and sister. He wants you to be there for them."

This woman was so stuck in her grief, I got the feeling from her son that she was not really present for her other kids.

" 'Shower them with love the way you did with me,' " I said. " 'And don't start up with the pills.' He is adamant about that. He says, 'Don't do what I did because you are sad!' That is what he wants to tell you."

The woman nodded.

"And he says not to let his brother hang out in bars. He doesn't want him making the same mistakes that he made," I said. I got the sense that his younger brother was partying hard to cope with his grief, and that this could lead him down the wrong path.

"Okay," she said. "I will pass along the message."

"He's not high anymore," I said. "Not on drugs, anyway...but on love. So remember to love and that he loves you so much."

The woman wept into her hands as her son stepped back into the light.

On another occasion, I had a young woman come to my office and tell me that a friend had died. She asked if I could hear anything from them that I could tell her. As I connected to that friend, I understood that the individual had crossed from a drug overdose. There was a tremendous amount of energy around this spirit as they communicated to this girl through me. Through the reading, he kept saying how proud he was of her and profusely saying to tell her that it was *not her fault.*

The thing that made her happiest was that he told her that he was in the light of God, how happy he was, and that he was drug-free. After the reading, she disclosed to me that they had both been drug users. When two drug addicts hang out together, it may not be because they like each other, but that they share a behavior, and they get their needs met by seeing the same behavior in the other person.

She recognized there would be no good ending if she kept up that behavior and had managed to get clean before he died. She stopped hanging out with him and didn't go to the places she knew he would go. When she told me this, I knew of course that this was in her best interest, but she felt terrible because he had gone on to overdose. He ended up where she might have herself, but she felt guilt for having disconnected from him, like she had abandoned him. I was glad that, hearing from him, she was able to have peace of mind, knowing that he was now alive in the light of God in a drug-free place, just like she was on this side.

In this country today, addiction is no joke. We have a terrible problem with it, and, in my line of work, it's coming up more and more that this is the way someone crossed. I did a show in Chicago where I was doing a reading for a woman and I said to her, "Your mother is telling me about your new baby, but she's saying something about how you had a hard time conceiving this child. She said you have babies on the other side that are with her in the light." The woman was grateful to hear this and was now crying. I told her, "There's something that I don't understand. There is someone standing with your mother who is trying to make it clear to me that she is definitely of a different race, and she's saying, 'Send my love to the baby.' " I didn't know why I was seeing this and why this particular thing was being stressed, that this individual was of a different race.

The woman then told me that she had been involved with social services that look after children, and that there was a mixed-race child, a little girl, whose mother had a lot of issues. The woman would always be called upon to look after the child when her mother abandoned her (which she did repeatedly). The mother was a drug addict and not reliable, but, whenever they'd go before the judge, the mother would clean up her act and the child would be put back with her. It was driving this woman crazy, because the little girl was kept in the middle of this terrible ongoing drama. Sadly, the little girl's mother passed away from a drug overdose. Afterward, this woman fought for custody of the little girl and won. Since then, the little girl has become her adopted daughter. The mother who passed away was standing next to the woman's mother, saying, "Thank you, and please tell my daughter I love her and I'm sorry."

If someone was a big drinker or did drugs and they died and haven't chosen to go into the light, they will hang around susceptible souls who are on earth and stay close to them. It's like getting a contact high. Many of these souls caused a lot of pain when they were alive, and they realize this when they cross over, so they're afraid of the light. When they get to the other side they think, "Now what's God going to do to me?" So they stay earthbound, looking for a body to occupy. They think, "I'm going to go hang out at the bars, and I'm going to antagonize these other people who are sitting here, and I'm going to feed off their energy and try to get buzzed from being around them."

You know that expression, "You weren't acting like yourself?" Sometimes it's true, because you have a lost soul hanging onto your energy. Souls can literally latch onto you if you compromise yourself by drinking or partying too much. I'm not saying you shouldn't be able to enjoy yourself or have a few drinks now and then. But if you overdo it one night (or several nights in a row), when you wake up bleary-eyed, look in the mirror and say this:

I command that any energy that has attached itself to me that is not for my highest good be gone, and go back to the light for healing. In the name of God, hear my prayer.

And then that dark energy has to leave. They can't stay if you kick them out.

In addition to the prayers, it's helpful to clear your space by burning sage. While sage used to be hard to find, now you can buy it at most grocery stores. It either comes in a bunch or loose-leaf, like a tea. When you light it, say a prayer and visualize the white light coming into each room. Open windows to let in fresh air, and be sure to walk through each room, hitting every corner. (Even the closets. I'm not kidding!) I do it after I have clients in my home, or perhaps after Thanksgiving dinner if someone had too much wine while watching football. It's a great way to reboot your space and keep negative energies at bay.

You can also say a prayer:

I bring in the white light to clear this space of any negative energy that is not for my highest good. Thank you in full faith.

The power of prayer is very real. I know this now, from all the work I've done with the dead. They do hear your prayers, and if they can't make it to your rescue, they will find some sort of angelic being who can.

Chapter 7

This Wouldn't Be Happening if You Couldn't Handle It

How often have we heard it said that God never gives us more than we can handle? Even though I have been very blessed in my life, I can say that this certainly doesn't always seem to be true. I see what many people go through in the course of a life and am constantly amazed at how strong a person can be. Experiencing grief is no sign of weakness. Our grief is as deep as our love, and it's pretty rare that we are granted love with no amount of grief to go along with it.

I say it all the time: the other side is complete peace, even bliss. There is no pain or sorrow. All is forgiven, all is love. This side is the tough place. This is where we are challenged to grow spiritually and come to understand and embrace our true godly nature.

As I talked about at more length in my last book, *Inside the Other Side*, before coming here, we basically signed a spiritual agreement for the life we were about to live. Or, to keep with the reality-show metaphor, we answered the producer's casting call and were a good fit for the role. Challenging lives help us grow spiritually: single parenting or parenting a special-needs kid, illness or incapacity, addiction, abuse, not having enough, trying to do something difficult, trying again and again, living with disappointment, wanting something we can't have this time, and loss—all these things, though they can be incredibly difficult and even painful, polish our soul's diamond.

I'm on the same path you are on. We start out knowing almost nothing, and little by little our eyes are opened. We all are one, yet until we have some painful experiences, we can't fully know another's pain. The tough times and losses we endure are lessons in empathy. The challenge is to let those experiences expand our hearts, rather than make them shrink with bitterness. (I admit there are some very loving souls who seem to be *born* with natural empathy, but I can tell you with certainty that these are old souls who've definitely had a good share of painful experiences in past lifetimes.)

When my brother Harold passed, he was the first person in my immediate family to go. I didn't lose my father until ten years later, and my mother passed another eight years after my father. But with Harold leaving, it was like I experienced for the first time what others in my neighborhood were feeling, the ones who'd been coming to me to ask for some word from their loved ones who had crossed. Before that, I could never quite grasp why people would be so desperate to know that their loved one who had passed was okay. I just had never experienced that kind of loss. Losing my brother was a major lesson in empathy.

When we are struggling here, the thing that we all lose sight of is that we *chose* to come back to the earth plane, and that we *chose* to undergo certain challenges. We do not know every single thing that will happen to us in the life we're about to live before we sign our new spiritual contract, because here on the earth plane we have free will and can alter our course at any time. But we definitely are given some sense of the level of difficulty and have agreed to it. Karma is always involved. At some point before we can "graduate" spiritually, we need to balance negative karma that we've created for ourselves with our past actions and behavior. While we might have the choice to skip something hard in one new lifetime here, at some point we'll have to address it and set things right. We might even, before coming here, agree to take on something extremely difficult just because we understand how much growth it will create for us.

Many people I talk with in my work tell me terrible stories, stories that are just so sad, or simply bewildering and hurtful. They want to know *why*. Why would God bring this person into my life and then take them away? Why do I have this illness or disability? Why was I born into a family that I just don't mesh with and can't seem to get along with, no matter how hard I try? Why do I always seem to attract the person who treats me badly? Or, one of the saddest of all, how could my child die before me?

I have wondered about these same questions myself: *God, what were you thinking???* The truth is, I do not know. But I do know that there is a reason. And I do know that karma is not punishment. When we are here, we cannot fathom why terrible things would happen to us or to others we care about. But I do know that each of us, when we get to the other side again, is fully aware of the reasons for everything that happens in our life here. We need to trust that. We were not sent here to suffer randomly. We came here to learn and grow. The expression "growing pains" didn't come out of nowhere.

One thing that I'm very concerned about right now is the opioid addiction problem we're having in our country. I talked about it in the last chapter, but I have never seen anything comparable to it in my life and career. I admit it really scares me, even though I know there is a reason for it.

Just this past week, a close friend of mine told me about the death of a young girl, twenty-one years old, who was best friends with her daughter. She had been involved with drugs before, but her family was feeling very hopeful, as she had been clean for the past four or five months. Then her parents found her unconscious. My friend showed me her photo, and you wouldn't believe how beautiful she was, like an angel. Gorgeous green

eyes, lovely personality, she said. Just an amazing, lovely, poor
thing. Apparently she'd relapsed on her sobriety and sadly
had gotten hold of a bad batch of fentanyl. Now her family is
experiencing such horror and devastation. My girlfriend, who is
an angel on earth, is taking care of all the funeral arrangements
because the mother is an emotional wreck and cannot manage.
Already the mother is struggling with questions like, "Where is
she?" and "What more could I have done?"

When the girl was taken unconscious from the home, she was
brain-dead, but she was kept alive at the hospital for a time
because she had signed up to be an organ donor. Strangely, about
a week before she died, she had said, "If anything happens to
me, please make sure that they follow through with my organ
donations." What twenty-one-year-old says that? I know the kid
had a premonition. The mother sat vigil with her daughter on life
support, hoping that by some miracle her daughter would come
back to life—that's the state of mind she was in. Of course that
didn't happen, but, after the organs had been donated to others
whose lives could be saved and life support was turned off, the
mother told my friend that, once they were back in their home,
all the lights went off and then back on, then off, then back on,
several times. The mother was so stricken, thinking it could be
a sign from her daughter. They live in a condominium complex,
and she went to her neighbors to ask if their lights had gone off,
thinking maybe there was a power surge or something. But her
neighbors all told her their lights had not gone off. I believe that
the daughter was letting her mother know that she was home
with God on the other side and that all was well with her.

These really are such scary times. This poor girl was the fourth
kid in her town around this same age who died of this kind of
overdose. It is tragic for every person whose life is touched by

this terrible, heartbreaking scourge, but I know that the reason this is happening is karmic at its roots. It's not just individual people who have karma. As groups, even nations, we have karma, too. This issue is happening massively, all around us, so it has to do with all of us in some way. We have some re-balancing to do to solve this problem, that is for sure. We all need to be strong, and we need to be there for each other.

On both sides of the veil (especially this one), we need to get over playing the game of shame and blame. Over there, it doesn't last long, once we get past our life review. When reviewing all our past actions, we may experience a sense of shame or disappointment in ourselves, and that fresh awareness will inspire us to try to make better choices in our next lifetime. Also, even while still on that side, a spirit may want to take any opportunity to apologize when they know they have done wrong, or try to give extra assistance to someone here they feel a debt toward.

I do believe that shame has a purpose on this side of the veil. It can remind us that we have higher standards for ourselves and make us recognize that we did not live up to them. Shame is a reminder to try to do better. Just bear in mind that a little bit of it goes a long way. We don't need to take it to the furthest lengths. If we let down a friend or really hurt someone, either physically or by spreading gossip or something similar, then we should feel some guilt and shame and make sure we step up our game. We need to apologize, and we may have some repair work to do in a relationship. But in all honesty, I can feel guilty if I even take too many Splendas at the Dunkin', so sometimes I have to remind myself to reel it in.

One thing I hear over and over is the guilt and extra grief some people experience when their loved one dies in the hospital and they are not there to say a last goodbye. You may have stayed with your husband, or wife, or child, day in and day out. You've talked to them, read to them, gone without meals, without rest, without showering. Then, it seems, the moment you left for a break is when your loved one passed away.

I understand how this can seem like you were falling down on the job, as if you didn't care quite enough, weren't quite strong enough, were too self-absorbed. But please know this is not the case.

This happens to so many people. I know. It happened to me.

At the end of his life, my father was in the hospital. I had been visiting him, and he looked perfectly fine. He was going to be moved to a different room the next day. As I was leaving, planning to return the next day, he said to me, "I never want to be a burden to your mother or to the family." It was heartbreaking because I knew he was saying farewell. But because he looked well, I didn't see any reason to worry that he was going to die. The next day, before I could return, he was gone.

Think back to when you were a little kid and you were about to be left with a babysitter. Your parents would always try to distract you with something so that you wouldn't notice that they'd slipped out the back door. They didn't want to upset you. It's like that when it's time to cross. Many souls who are really ready to go hang on while their living loved ones are near and seem to need them not to go yet. Again, they don't want to upset you. So they wait until you are not there to cross. The biggest gift you can give someone you truly care about who needs to cross is your permission and your blessing. Tell them it's okay to go. Tell them that you love them. Tell them you will see them again. (You will!) Over and over in readings, I will hear from spirits that they heard and appreciated that their loved ones here told them that they understood and wanted them to do what was best for them. That it was okay to go. There is absolutely no reason to feel shame or blame for missing the moment your loved one crosses. They are honestly trying to spare you.

Some months back, I did a reading for a woman at my home. She was recently widowed, and, when her husband died, she became a single mother to four children, so it was very sad. Her husband had been very sick and was in the hospital. She'd been sitting with him for long stretches at a time but had gone home to take a shower and change her clothes before going right back.

As she was getting dressed after her shower, a blue jay landed on her bedroom windowsill and looked directly at her. The window was closed, so she wasn't sure it could actually see her, since there was probably a glare on the pane. But even if the bird could not actually see her, it could certainly see a motion inside, and a bird will usually fly away if someone approaches it. Nevertheless, as she moved toward the window, the bird did not budge. She was able to get right up close and exchange a long look with the bird. Then she felt a light breeze blow over her as she stood there in the house, with the window still closed, and suddenly had a premonition that her husband had passed.

At that moment her phone rang—it was the hospital telling her that her husband had indeed passed away. It was very quick. No one had told her that her husband was near to dying, even though she knew he was really sick.

Through tears, she asked me if I thought that bird had come to prepare her for the news. I said yes, that was her husband's way of telling her that he was free and was not going to be restricted any more. She already believed that, but she wanted "expert" confirmation. It didn't make her loss easier—this was her life partner and the father of her children—but through her grief, she had that moment to hold onto and remember.

I had a client who had a six-year-old daughter. When her mother—the little girl's grandmother—passed away, my client missed her very much and for a long time was consumed by grief. Her mother had been a big part of their lives and had enjoyed a special bond with her granddaughter, calling her "my little princess." And the little girl had absorbed some of her grandmother's examples of strength. When her mother was crying, the little girl would say, "Don't cry, Mother! We're *warriors*, not worriers," an expression she had heard her grandmother use often. But still my client couldn't seem to get over her grief.

From time to time, her daughter would say that she'd seen her grandmother. My client would ask, "Where was she? Where did you see her?"

And her daughter would say, "Oh, she was in the yard," or, "I saw her in the car." But my client believed her daughter was just trying to cheer her up—she never thought her daughter had actually seen her mother, so when she asked her those questions, she was just "playing along."

Finally she took hold of herself. She told me, "I realized, I had to get a grip. It wasn't fair, what I was doing to my family. My own daughter, just six years old, is trying to keep me—her mother—

together. I'm the adult here; I need to act like it." She reached out to her mother, as she had often during her grieving, to talk to her. She told her she was going to try to stop her crying and move forward with her life. She said, "All I ask is that you watch over my daughter, your little princess, and keep her safe."

A short time later, she drove her daughter to a birthday party for one of her little friends and collected her afterward to go home. She cleared the back seat of the car of the toys and party favors her daughter had brought home, giving it a thorough sweep.

The next day, as she situated her daughter in the back seat so that they could go grocery shopping, the mother found a child's plastic tiara. She had no idea where it could have come from, as she knew she hadn't left anything in the car. When she picked it up, she saw written on the front, "Little Princess." Immediately she was swept with a feeling of love and gratitude, knowing that her mother was not gone and that her spirit would be looking after her granddaughter, just as she'd asked.

Sometimes our struggle on this side of the veil can be just getting along with a problematic family member. Most of us have an ideal in mind of the perfect family relationship, siblings who have each other's backs, parents who care for and support their children, always looking out for their best interests. We might even know families that seem, at least from the outside, to be perfect in these ways. But many of us have family relationships that fall far short of that. I've had my own in-law dramas, to the point where my mother-in-law is more of a Mother Outlaw (at least to me). Until we get to the other side, it can be a total mystery why we have the relationships we do, but each of us can try to make things better.

A woman about my age came to see me one time, a few years ago. She apparently had had difficulty with her sister their entire lives. The two just never got along. This woman seemed to me to be caring and nice, but she described her sister as rough and disagreeable and said they were polar opposites. I don't recall the whole story or what, if any, involvement there was from their mother, but she said that it was their father who was always trying to make peace between them. That may have worked to a degree while he was still alive, but after their father passed, the sisters had a big falling-out. The sister had even insulted my client's children, which really crossed a line for her. But after this incident, she'd had a dream in which her father was again encouraging her to try to make peace with her sister. She knew this was the right thing to do but was torn because it just seemed hopeless. They'd never been on the same page. So even though the dream was compelling, she got up the next morning and went downstairs feeling unconvinced. Maybe her father was wrong and she should just write off her sister for good.

While she was sipping her coffee, she absent-mindedly went over and turned on the TV, without having any idea of what she wanted to watch. The channel that came on was broadcasting classic sitcoms, and what should she see but *Father Knows Best*. She smiled, realizing that it was a sign, and resolved to make yet another go with her sister.

The folks on the other side can't totally clue you in and can't give you a free pass, so you won't have to experience these painful karmic situations. This is all between you and the big guy upstairs, and you work through it with your fellow "cast members," here in your own reality show. But know that the spirits are here to look out for you and give you comfort and help in any way that presents itself, even if it's only to let you know that they are nearby.

Many times I've seen someone who has crossed desperately wanting to reach out to those left here, especially when they are aware that their loved ones won't understand something about their crossing, or might feel in some way at fault. They never want us to be sad, but to live our lives fully and find joy, even when we miss them terribly. In the case of suicide, a very common worry for those left here is that their loved one will somehow be punished on the other side. I want everyone to know, that's not how God operates. While the soul in question may be disappointed for themselves if, upon reflection, they know they could have made another choice, God is all-forgiving. That soul will have another chance to come back and wrestle again with their karma on this side, but while on the other side they experience total love, total acceptance, total peace.

At one of my shows, I did a reading for a woman whose son had committed suicide. She was devastated, fearing he might not be in heaven. I told her that he certainly was in heaven, and I was able to give her enough validating information that she was confident she was really hearing from him, and that he was, in fact, well on the other side. Among the messages he gave me for his mother was a sign he kept showing me that said, "Thank you, please come again." I asked the mother what this sign could possibly mean. She had been very upset, but suddenly she laughed. She told me she had said to a friend when she was coming to the show that, if she got information she felt was legitimate from this evening, she would certainly come again— but *only* if she got information from me that let her know for sure it was really her son. Apparently she was convinced, and her son was aware of her earlier comment. He also must have had a sense of humor. I said to her, " 'Thank you, please come again.' " She cracked up. It was so cute.

As a medium, I'm aware that many people think I know everything that's going to happen. They may even expect that I can prevent something bad from happening, or at least sound an alarm. I'm not God—not even close—so the power to prevent bad things (which should almost always be read as "karmic" things) from happening is not in my hands. And many times, I don't know enough even to give a heads-up. I think of 9/11 as a good example. For sure, before the terrible attacks happened back in 2001, I was aware that there was something truly awful coming. I could feel the energy, as if the very air was thickening, but I honestly did not know what was on its way. And no, there was nothing I could do about it. I was as torn-up in the aftermath as everyone else was. That's one of the hardest things about having this ability, not to be able to help when I truly want to. As much as I feel blessed with this life, that is a real downside.

Living with this ability as a child, I recall having friends in school that I knew were not going to make it in life, or who had stuff going on at home, but couldn't talk about it. I would be aware of souls around them, and hear…"little secrets," you might call them. I remember not knowing how to deal with that, how to handle it. I didn't even tell my mother and father about this, because I had enough issues of my own when I was an adolescent without bringing up these other things I knew.

When I was in third grade, our class put on a play. I was, as usual, making myself the center of attention, organizing everything, deciding who was going to be what, and arranging for costumes. A boy from our class came up to me and said, "I can help you get costumes—I have costumes at home." The minute he said this to me, I looked at him. I never got attention from boys at eight or nine years old, so this was all new to me. But it wasn't that. It was that when I looked at him, I felt a great energy of sadness around him, a tremendous sadness. If I had to say it today, I would say that I knew he wasn't going to live long. But at that age, I couldn't put my finger on it; I just knew there was something tragic about him. Long story short, a few years went by, we were in eighth grade, junior high. This boy became a football player. He was going out with a girl and she broke up with him, and he went home and shot himself in the head. I will never forget this as one of the first times I knew something that I couldn't quite put my finger on, but still *knew* it. Today I live in a town right next to where I lived as a kid, and every time I drive down the street where he used to live, I always think of that poor boy and say a silent prayer for him.

Back in those days, we were really less aware about the emotional states of our peers. There is still a terrible problem with young people and suicide, and I think that the bullying that kids do on social media has exacerbated this to a degree. But if I was a kid today and had such a bad feeling about someone I knew, I might have the presence of mind to let a teacher know of my concerns, or he might have known to call a suicide hotline. I don't think those even existed when I was in school. So maybe we have made a little progress, at least.

A lot of times when we think of terrible loss, especially when talking about psychically connecting with spirits, the only kind of loss we think of is someone who has crossed to the other side. But the loss of someone who is still "here" can be just as painful, sometimes more so, and is often something we experience well before we lose someone close to us through death. The strong connections we make here almost always have a karmic component—that's what makes them matter; it's like karma is a kind of glue that binds us. This can take all different kinds of shapes. I've had girlfriends who, when they break up with a guy, literally hate his guts and never want to see him again. I've had girlfriends who tend to stay friendly with their past lovers. But all these relationships supposedly started out of a strong attraction and included love at some point. Whatever went down, some kind of karmic debt was discharged in the relationship. And because of the importance of the bond, there can be very strong feelings of loss when a love relationship ends, equal even to that person dying. In some cases, it can almost be more crushing to know that the person you lost or let go of is still here, forming other relationships that you are not part of. It can hurt like hell!

One of my girlfriends told me that the day she signed her divorce papers was the saddest day of her entire life. There were very good, insurmountable reasons why she and her husband were breaking up. But they were karmically bound, and she believed she would be with him again in another life. Meanwhile, she'd have to see him enjoying another marriage, having children, raising them, and so forth, all without her.

Earlier I talked about my first true love, Sam, and how we eventually broke up, in spite of sharing a deep and passionate love. I can honestly say this was one of the most painful experiences of my life. Any time I ever heard a song like Bonnie Raitt's "I Can't Make You Love Me," I would feel a pang for what could have been. The Barbra Streisand and Robert Redford movie *The Way We Were* came out when we were dating and we saw it together. I knew even then that someday we'd be having a version of that sad ending. And of course, afterward, any time I saw any reference to that movie, I couldn't help but remember the way *we* were. It was like a tattoo on my heart. It was a pain that went to the depths of my soul and lasted for many years. Like a death, it was something that I just had to find a way, somehow, to live with.

I want you to know that, as hard as it is, you *can* live with these kinds of losses. You can go forward and survive, and even eventually thrive, after a broken heart. Barbra Streisand's character was completely heartbroken losing that relationship, even though she could see that it was never going to work. But in its wake, she became who she was supposed to be.

Around the world, there are endless tragedies—fires, hurricanes, epidemics, starvation. Nobody gets away without experiencing pain in some form. But, whenever possible, we can try to meet these experiences with a willingness to comfort and soothe one another, to spread our wings of compassion, and maybe even be inspired by another's resilience or courage. Fred Guttenberg, who lost his daughter, Jaime, in the Parkland school shooting, has made it his mission to fight for gun control to honor his daughter and prevent this tragedy happening to another family. The mother who lost her daughter to drugs might remember her daughter's generous soul, the girl who had decided she wanted to be an organ donor, and maybe she will decide to do something that will honor her memory of her daughter.

Through all our trials, we need to take time for some tears, and then rise to the occasion. Pull strength from within and from your own God Squad on the other side. You can do it. You can burn the whole frickin' house down. But as long as you come out of the ashes, you will be all right. Just call on the angels for the strength you need—they are there waiting for you to ask them.

Chapter 8

How May I Help You?

The spirits of our loved ones on the other side love to assist us any way they can. They just love to help out—they really get a kick out of it. I always tell people to ask for help—ask for anything. It can be something important or something trivial; it doesn't matter. They can protect you from danger, locate a missing document, or make you a baloney sandwich. Okay, maybe not the baloney sandwich, but...you just never know.

One thing in dealing with the dead is that you have to be clear about your intentions. You can't leave them guessing. You can't say, "I'd like a baloney sandwich," and then go, "but I probably should just have a salad," and then, "No, what I'd *really* like is a bowl of ice cream—how many points is that?" Yes, the dead have an eternity, but they don't have time for *that!* You need to be sure you want that baloney sandwich and then clearly ask for just that.

I see uncertainty among my clients, both women and men. Someone will say that they'd like to meet someone and get married, but then they aren't sure, for whatever reason. They're not sure they are over their last relationship or not sure they want to change their lifestyle. I tell them, "When you make up your mind, *then* ask your folks on the other side. But make up your mind first."

I frequently am hired to do a party or a private group reading. About three years ago, I did one of these in a town not too far from where I live. A woman in the group I was reading for was bemoaning her love life and how her last so-called boyfriend had been a big fat idiot. But she was very sure that she wanted to move on and find love again (no switching from baloney sandwich to salad!), and right away I heard from her folks on the other side, telling her that something much better was coming her way. I heard specifically the name "Mike." I told her this and I said to her, "Don't worry—he's not going to be like that other *mamaluke* you're just getting over!" I suggested that she try saying a prayer, making her desires clear to the universe—by which I really mean, making her intentions clear to the folks on the other side. A short time later, she and some of her friends were down at the shore, in Belmar, having a meal at a pizza place called Mamalukes. Who should she meet but a very nice guy named Mike. And...they are now married.

I cannot tell you how often I ask for help from the other side when I can't find something. In one of my other books, I told the story of how John had lost his keys in a yard full of snow, but I was able to go straight to them once I asked the folks on the other side for directions. This is an area where they really seem to excel!

My brother Harold has constantly been a great dispatcher for me. When all else fails, I always call on him. He's just amazing. I feel like he is very highly evolved. And he listens. Every time I call him for something—whether it's to find a piece of paper, locate my keys, or just a blouse I put away last summer that I can't find—he's always there and always helps me. I don't ask for crazy things like the winning lottery numbers. I know better than that. But for simple things I always ask for his help, and he does not let me down.

I was on Facebook a short while ago, and I noticed someone I recognized from "the olden days" of the early 1970s had posted a photo of themselves and another person I also recognized. I was so thrilled to see these two people in the photo because I knew them both, and I was thinking to myself, *I know I have a picture, too, from right around that time, and I know where the picture is. I'm going to post it and ask, "Do you remember this?"* So I went into the storage space where I keep these old, old photographs from before I was married. The photos were gone. I could not find them. I knew they should be there, because I'd always kept them where I could put my hands on them, but...*nada.*

I tore the storage space apart. Not only did I tear it apart, I thought I hurt my back—I'd gotten so frantic in my efforts, thinking that the photos were lost or thrown out, or who knows what happened to them. I was practically throwing things up in the air like a cartoon, trying to find those pictures. Poor John was going through his stuff at the other end of the storage area, throwing me looks and trying to get me to calm down while I'm acting like an absolute maniac. Finally I realized: those photos were my baloney sandwich.

I stopped and took a deep breath. Then I said to my dear friend Roy, who is passed away (I'll say more about him later), and my dear beloved brother Harold, "Please tell me these photos aren't gone. They mean so much to me. Please help me find them."

I had someone, years ago, whom I was dating, steal photos from me, so I have experienced that pain of knowing something that is never going to be replaced is gone forever. Photos are like your history; losing them can be really awful. So I said my prayer to Roy and Harold, and it wasn't more than ten minutes before I had my hands on the photograph album. I was tickled because I had looked in the same spot (or so I'd thought) at least seven times! But there it was, and I was just so thrilled.

Later, after I'd done my post, I went upstairs and was on the phone talking with a girlfriend, while at the same time I was looking in the closet for something else—seems like I'm always looking for something! And, while I was looking in the closet, I suddenly realized there was somebody standing next to me. I literally jumped in alarm because John had gone out and I knew there was nobody in the house but me. I could tell there was "nobody" actually there, but it was a male energy. As I jumped, my girlfriend on the phone said, "What's the matter?"

I said, "Oh my God. It was my brother. He was just standing right next to me as I'm looking in the closet."

And my girlfriend said, "Well, maybe he was trying to tell you he was happy he was *out* of the closet!" We both laughed.

I get such a thrill whenever I see someone else do this trick of asking their deceased loved ones for help. I was at my favorite restaurant in Boonton the other night, Top of the Park, where I run into many folks I know from town and am frequently recognized. Again last night I ran into a woman who reminded me that we'd had a meeting together. She wanted to express to me how grateful she was that I taught her how to look for something when she loses it. She said, "I had a baby's bracelet that I was saving for my daughter. It was hers when she was a baby and I wanted to give it to her when she had a baby of her own. But I hadn't looked for it in a long time." Of course, when she wanted it, she couldn't put her hand on it. She had no idea where she'd put it. She turned the house upside down and went through every single box, but couldn't find it. After hours of searching, she was completely discouraged and figured she must, at some point, have given it away and just didn't remember, or else it was simply lost for good.

Then she remembered to ask the way I had told her: "When you are looking for something you can't find, call on your mother (who had passed away) and ask her for any help you need."

She said, "Concetta, I did as you said, and even added, 'In the name of God, hear my prayer.' It was not even half an hour later that I found the bracelet. I was so happy. I felt like my mother was standing right there." I assured her that she was.

Another thing the dead are good at, as I've said before, is manipulating electricity, whether they are just letting you know they are there or whether they are doing something helpful. The spirits are made entirely of energy themselves, and anything electrical can be influenced, from lights in the home to smartphones to digital clocks.

A client of mine had lost her father about six months earlier. They'd had a close relationship, but one bone of contention between them was that, even though he was ninety and had had a few incidents of losing consciousness while walking (due to a heart condition, for which he'd gotten a pacemaker), he refused to give up the car keys and stop driving. She and her brother had tried reasoning with him and had even spoken with the local police, who told them nothing could be done; his license was valid and, unless he did something dangerous or unlawful, they could not prohibit him from driving. They were terrified he would have an accident and hurt or kill himself—or somebody else—but he was stubborn. Fortunately, nothing came of their fears before their father passed away, shortly before his ninety-first birthday.

My client's mother was in a nursing home in another state, and she and her boyfriend went to visit her and take her to lunch for Mother's Day. When they drove home to New York (more than seven hours of driving round-trip), she was hoping to get a parking spot on her block. There was a spot, but it was at the end of a school lane, and you weren't really supposed to park there. People who lived on her block commonly did park there since the lane was never used, but her boyfriend didn't like for her to park there because it wasn't legal. He warned her that, one of these days, she would get a ticket if she did. But after the long drive, she convinced him to just let her park there overnight, and she would move the car in the morning.

Early the next day, the two went out for a run. She planned to move the car when they got back and her boyfriend left for work. As they jogged down the block, she said to him, "Man, look at all these great parking spots! I should have brought the key down with me. I hope there'll be a good one left when we get back." As they neared her car (a Prius hybrid), parked in the school lane, it suddenly turned on!

Her boyfriend turned to her and said, "Oh, so you *did* bring the key."

She said, "No, I didn't! I didn't turn on the car. Are you sure that *you* don't have the key?" He said that no, he didn't; he actually thought she was joking with him and that she really had the key, but she turned her pockets inside out to show him she did not. Nevertheless, the car was on, so he got in and re-parked it before they went for their run.

She couldn't get over what had just happened. She'd had the car for several years, and nothing like that had ever happened before. She googled it to see if this was common with the half-electric car and found only one other person describing her car spontaneously turning on, and in the comments thread everyone said this shouldn't happen—one person even said they thought her post was just a prank. Then one other thought came to mind, and she called me to tell me what had occurred. She said, "Concetta, it was just uncanny. I was just saying it was too bad I hadn't brought my key with me and then—right then—my car turned itself on. I was always arguing with my dad about the car keys. Do you think...?"

I said, "Without a doubt! You can thank your father for helping you out, moving your car."

Sometimes the only help we really need from the other side is to be comforted. I recall having a terrible dream that I was on a ship and it was storming and there were huge waves coming up over the portholes. I was terrified that the ship would capsize and I would drown. (Even being a Jersey Girl and loving the beach, I've always had a fear of drowning, which I believe must come from a past life.) I suffer from anxiety and so was getting really panic-stricken, my heart beating so fast. But in my dream, I heard my father whisper to me. He was saying very gently and calmly, "You're not on the boat. You're not on the boat." Hearing his voice, I became conscious that I was dreaming and I was not in danger. I was safe. It was just a dream.

I had a woman come for a reading who wanted to hear from her mother. Her mother came through with many wonderful messages, telling my client about her own life and her past. One of the things she told her about was from when she was a little girl at her grandmother's house in a rural, farm-like area. The grandmother used to bring a wicker basket of laundry to the backyard, and the little girl used to help her grandmother and mother hang the clothes on the line to dry. It was sweet for her to remember this. Then, when I was doing the reading, her mother also said, "Thank you for the roses." My client told me how her mother had always loved roses, and she and other family members had known that to bring her roses when they visited would make her happy. But then her mother said, "I sent the rose." The woman at first wasn't sure what she meant by this, but after the reading was over I could see on her face that she'd had a realization. She proceeded to tell me that when her grandson was sick and in the hospital, they were having trouble diagnosing exactly what was wrong with him. The family was in a panic because, whatever it was, he seemed to be getting worse. She'd called upon her mother and asked her to please help the boy. The next time she went back to the hospital to visit the boy, she saw that they were getting ready to release him. He was well, and they never did figure out what was wrong with him. When she'd gone into the boy's room, she'd been delighted to see that he had recovered. On the table at the side of the bed, she saw one red rose.

She'd asked the boy, "Who gave you the rose?" He didn't know, and nobody else seemed to know where the flower had come from. Now the mystery was solved!

Here is a story that I really love because it happened to someone very dear to me. When my friend got married, she was all in to be part of her husband's family. And all through her marriage she and her mother-in-law got along really well. They liked and respected each other and simply had a great relationship. But where her mother-in-law was sweet and kind to her, her father-in-law for some reason treated her like an outsider. He never had a kind word for her, no matter what she did, and showed no appreciation for anything she contributed, whether it was a cooked meal for the family or a gift. It was just horrible for my friend, who only wanted harmony.

Then, sadly, her mother-in-law, whom she dearly loved, passed away.

But once she was over there on the other side, it seemed her mother-in-law could not wait to set things right! In a reading I did for my friend and her husband, his mother came through loud and clear and told the two she was sad about the poor treatment my friend was receiving. So both she and her husband knew without doubt how his mother felt. Still, they never said anything to his father, probably considering it a lost cause.

But the strange thing was, even though *he* never said a word to confirm this, she and her husband believe that the mother-in-law was also talking to her husband! Little by little, his attitude seemed to completely change toward his daughter-in-law. He began treating her like a real daughter for the first time ever. He began to give her little gifts, such as jewelry and little objects that his wife had once owned and adored, telling her, "I know she would want you to have this." I jokingly remarked that I thought he might have been visited by a Ghost of Christmas Past!

By the time he himself passed away, the two of them were very close and very friendly. The change was utterly amazing. We couldn't help but believe that it was all due to his wife's spirit coming to him in defense of the daughter-in-law she loved, telling him he had better shape up and change his ways!

I love this story—in this case the other side did not just give a small assist but, I believe, changed many lives by giving someone much-needed advice and perspective.

A young man came to me at my office. He had been raised by
an abusive father, and, to my surprise, this is whom he asked to
hear from. The father did come through, and over and over he
expressed to this young man how he wished he had done better,
made better choices. He said that the strongest regret of his
life was how he acted as a father. He mentioned a few specific
things, mistakes he had made, which this young man recognized
and confirmed. Then I said to him, "Your father is giving you
suggestions on how to be a good father. He's suggesting that even
if you are helping out with your brother's kids, you can still be a
good role model. Even if you are working with other kids who are
not your own, you can be a father figure that kids can look up to."

I knew nothing of this man or why his father would be dispensing
this advice. (I assumed it was because he didn't want his son to
repeat mistakes he had made.) My client certainly looked old
enough that he could have kids of his own, but he never said
anything to me, other than telling me that he was connecting
with his father's words. He later got back to me to tell me more
of the story. He said that he was married to a woman who had a
little boy from a previous relationship, and that she had told him
she did not want more children. He was feeling resentful about
that because he would never have a child that was his own blood.
He told me that he understood his father was telling him those
things because, due to his resentment, he was not being nice to
his little stepson. He ended up telling me that hearing from his
dad had changed his life. He grasped that he had an opportunity
to be different from the way his father had been toward him,
and an opportunity to make a difference in a positive way in
this child's life. He told me that, after hearing from his father,
he decided, "I'm going to choose to be a better male role model
in this little boy's life." And, he said, his efforts were recognized

and appreciated almost immediately by this little boy. He wanted to thank me and say how grateful he was. I was delighted to hear his story, but he really was thanking his own father. And I like to think that this young man broke what could have been a disastrous chain, perpetuating the abuse he himself experienced, had he not been able to hear his dad and choose more wisely.

Earlier I spoke about a handful of times when I was protected by the other side giving me a warning about a person or a place I did not belong. This happens more often than you might realize, and you don't have to be psychic to get this kind of warning. Everyone, to at least some degree, has the sixth sense, the ability to physically or mentally sense things that they "can't really see" or "can't really know." Pretty much everyone, for example, has had the experience of feeling someone's eyes on them. You've had this experience, right? Of course you can't literally feel somebody's eyes on your body, but you can *sense*—with certainty—that someone is looking at you, even if they are behind your back. Or you have had a queasy sensation in your stomach that immediately makes you think that something is off, that a person is unsafe or maybe unethical, or will in some way be bad for you. These are feelings that you need to pay close attention to, as they are literally the other side giving you an alert.

Often, when we have one of these uncanny feelings, we might later say to a friend, "Something just told me" that it wasn't safe to go in there, or not to trust that person. Well, guess what? It isn't some*thing* that told you, it was some*one*.

I haven't talked a lot about this, since mostly in my books I'm giving shout-outs to the dead guys, but even more powerful than the spirits, and like a big spiritual blanket that offers us warmth and comfort, is the Holy Spirit itself.

My stepdaughter Jessica's daughter Isabella needs to have surgery for scoliosis. Jessica is a nervous wreck, and really all of us have been very, very worried about her. We've been going through the usual rounds of seeing doctors for the past few months and getting all the opinions. Her scoliosis is one of the worst cases I've ever seen. I've told Jessica to say some prayers and always remember to say, "In the name of God, hear my prayer."

Today she called me up and said, "I'm sending you a link." Princess Eugenie had just gotten married. She wore a wedding gown that exposed her upper back, clearly showing the scar from her scoliosis surgery.

In the interview, Eugenie said, "I want to give other people courage to know that there is good in doctors and hospitals—I've been cured. I want anyone out there to know that they can get the help they need." Jessica was so relieved to see the article. It gave her a great deal of peace and strength for what lies ahead for her daughter. I thoroughly believe that this is the Holy Spirit working through this young princess. Whenever someone takes on a challenge simply in order to inspire courage in others, or reveals some truth about themselves simply to offer comfort to another, to me that is the work of the Holy Spirit, a.k.a. God. This is God's work.

Chapter 9

AIR: Always in Reach

How much happier would we all be if we could understand that our loved ones who are no longer here with us in the flesh are still *very much* with us, all the time? Well, they are.

I'm not here to do a commercial for myself or other mediums, but I do think that's why a lot of people want to have a reading, why I'm booked up far in advance, and why my shows are always full. People are really hungry to have this knowledge that those they've loved, who are no longer in the flesh, are still alive, that "dead" is not dead. As my chapter title gives away, I always tell people that their deceased loved ones are Always. In. Reach. AIR—they are literally in the air we breathe. (I have to confess that I stole this acronym from my very good friend, Ginger, whom I mentioned earlier. She is an incredible fount of spiritual wisdom and has taught me so much.)

So many of my clients are concerned about trying to figure it all out, trying to reach their loved one in the "right" way. While I'm doing the reading or chatting with them, they are busy writing down every word I say. They want to get it perfect—how to connect with God, how to connect with their deceased loved one. They ask, "Where are they?" Or they ask me if they are "doing it right" when they pray. I understand this. I'm supposedly the expert. But the truth is we're all experts when it comes to those we love and who love us unconditionally. I love to tell them the truth: The right way to connect with the spirit of a loved one is to *do whatever turns you on*. Do what you feel comfortable doing. You can't do it wrong. Nobody is judging. While our understanding of it may have been suppressed for a very long time, there is a natural connection between us here in material form and those in spirit form on the other side. And they are as eager to connect with you as you are to connect with them.

It's really as easy as going for coffee with a friend or having dinner with a group. When you're with friends you talk easily, right? Well, connecting with the spirit of someone who has crossed to the other side can be just as easy. Pray as if you are talking to a close friend, or just *talk* to the spirit you want to reach. I talk to my God Squad all the time. If I'm going to do something important that I have some concerns about, I might ask them to be with me, and just by asking, I know they will be there. It takes the pressure and worry off my mind. Your conversation or request can be out loud or simply a thought in your head. They can hear it either way.

I will repeat what I said in the last chapter: You need to be clear about your intentions and not send the other side a mixed message. If you really want some sign from your loved one, but at the same time are really afraid of anything like that happening, then it probably won't happen. They do not want to scare you.

A client came to me very upset because her mother had passed away after being very sick. They had been very close and she'd hoped to have some sign from her mother that all was well with her on the other side. At the same time, she confessed to me that she was a little nervous about the possibility that someone who had passed on could contact her on this side. She was obviously conflicted, and that was having a negative effect on any ability her mother's spirit might have to be able to get through to her. I said to her, "This is what you need to do. You need to tell your mother, 'I am not afraid.' And you have to mean it! If you show her that you are afraid to hear from her, she won't reach out. The spirits are quite sensitive to our emotional state, and she won't want to frighten you." I added, "You can also say, 'In the name of God, please show me a sign.' Then keep your eyes, ears, and heart open. I feel confident that you will hear from your mother, or she will show you something to let you know she's around."

And as I've said many, many times, you need to be really paying attention for the signs! These can be something symbolic. Maybe there is an object that you connect with your loved one—you might see it in an unexpected place, or at a time that seems synchronistic. A sign could be numbers that you see repeatedly on a clock, for instance, or on a license plate or a street address. A sign could be something in nature—a bird, butterfly, a particular tree, flower, or rock—or something kooky that only you and your loved one would recognize as a sign—a particular cartoon character or a toothbrush of a particular color. It could be a song that was meaningful to both of you, or it can even be a scent, if your loved one wore a particular cologne or perfume or smoked a distinctive type of tobacco.

In the case of two women I read for last year, it was a symbol that was meaningful because of their country of origin. They were sisters, both so sweet. One of the sisters was blind. She was a wonderful, lovely mission entity—an advanced soul who is sent to be born on this side to accomplish a particular mission from God. She had such a beautiful and vibrant personality. During the session, the women told me that one of them had a son who married and bought a house, but he was very upset because his grandfather, whom he was close to, died before he could see the house. Apparently the grandfather was Irish, so the grandson had a big arrangement made in the shape of a four-leafed clover and sent to the funeral parlor. When he got to the funeral parlor, he told his family, "I'm disappointed—this didn't come out the way I wanted it to come out, it's not how I was picturing it. I'm just very disappointed."

After the service and the repast they went back to the house, and he again expressed his disappointment that his grandfather had not gotten to see the house. They don't know where it came from, or whose it was, but one of them happened to look down and saw on the floor a broken piece of ceramic that probably came from a dish. On the little piece were four-leafed clovers. So they understood this was a message from the grandfather: *"Grandson, I do see your house. I am here. And I'm proud of you."*

On another occasion, a woman told me that her grandmother died and the family went to put her ashes at Barnegat Bay. There were eight family members, and they each got a flower from a flower shop. Unfortunately, the shop only had seven white carnations and one pink. So they gave the pink one to the little granddaughter. They went to Barnegat Bay, put the ashes in the water, and then put the flowers in one by one before driving back to their house, which was on the water but a good distance from Barnegat Bay. When they were all sitting outside their home, they saw one pink carnation floating on the water. There was no way the flower could have traveled the distance from where the grandmother's ashes and the flowers had been put into the water. It could not have been the same pink carnation the little granddaughter had put in the water. But all were still amazed and considered this synchronicity a sign of acknowledgment from their grandmother.

I did a reading recently for a woman who started by saying that she had found my name in an unusual way and that she would tell me the details after our appointment. Here's what she shared:

Her daughter was graduating from college, and she sent her husband out to get a bouquet of flowers they would give to their daughter at the ceremony. Her husband was never that crazy about roses and wanted to get his daughter something a little different, a mixed bouquet, but when he got to the florists there were only two bouquets on offer—all roses. Without giving it much thought, he said, "Okay, I'll take them both." When he got home, my client asked him why he'd taken two and he simply said he didn't know; it had been impulsive. When the couple got to the stadium, it was really full. They spotted two available seats and grabbed them, sitting down next to a woman whose daughter was also graduating. They chatted a little while they waited for the ceremony to begin, and the woman shared that her husband had passed away. She was feeling emotional about the event, wishing he was there to witness it. She also felt bad because she had been so rushed that she had not had time to get flowers for her daughter. The couple right away offered her their extra bouquet, since they had two. At first she demurred, but they insisted, and, as the husband handed over one of the bouquets of roses, one of the flowers began to drop its petals as if the bouquet was trickling raindrops of color.

At this point the woman gasped and said, "Oh my God!" She then proceeded to tell my client that she had been to see a psychic— one Concetta Bertoldi—about a year earlier, who had told her that her husband had said he would give her a sign that he was there. The sign would be rose petals dropping and scattering like trickling rain.

Another client told me that her mother had passed away when my client was very young. Then her father became ill, and it was clear that he would not be around much longer. My client spoke by phone with her father on her birthday, and he asked her if she had received the card he sent. She hadn't; for whatever reason, the card had not arrived. For a time, whenever they spoke, he continued to ask, "Did you get the card yet?" but eventually they both gave up, just assuming it was forever lost in the mail. Then, four months before her next birthday, her dad passed away. On her birthday, the card he'd sent the previous year finally arrived in her mailbox.

I called on a woman who attended one of my shows recently in Fairfield, New Jersey. Her husband came through and said that there were some happy changes coming in her future. She started to cry and revealed that she'd just bought a new home and would be leaving the residence her husband had built for them. It was obviously an emotional move, and one that would be bittersweet for her. But her husband told her, "No matter where you go, I will go with you." Then he told me to ask his wife about the gold. When he said this, I could see him holding out a cupped hand, like he was holding something in it, so when I did as he asked, I made that same gesture to his wife. With that, the woman got out her phone and opened her photos. Right there was a picture she'd taken just that week. She had found some gold coins in the basement and she'd taken a picture of the coins, held in her hand, in that exact same gesture! For him to mention the gold that she had found, and to be able to show me how she held it in her hand, gave her a ton of reassurance that this was indeed her husband. She felt comforted about the move—that it was really the right thing to do and that her husband would be with her, no matter where she was living.

Oftentimes, the youngest among us is the most aware of the other side. When I did a reading for Teresa Giudice of *The Real Housewives of New Jersey* after her mother passed, I told her that one of her children was very sensitive and was seeing her mother, and this was confirmed. Her daughter had told her that she was seeing her grandmother's spirit. Another client had a four-year-old son whom she had put down for a nap, but he was crying and crying. She went to look in on him, but as she approached the door the crying had stopped, and, as she stepped into his room, she noticed he had his blanket pulled up over his head. She went to him and gently pulled down the blanket to see his face, which had a strange look on it. "What's the matter?" she asked him.

He replied, "The lady told me I was all right, but I was afraid of her."

"What lady?" she asked her son. "What did she look like?"

"She had blonde hair and was wearing a blue dress," he said. "I was afraid of her because I could tell she was a ghost." The woman was flabbergasted. Her son had described her mother, who was blonde, and in the only photo she still had of her, she wore a blue dress.

In yet another case, a husband and wife were at one of my shows, looking for their parents. As sometimes happens, both parents were talking at the same time from the other side. It's really hard when two souls talk at once, but I was doing my best to follow and try to fit together who was saying what to whom as I heard from both. I knew the parents of this couple were trying to talk about their grandchildren. I said, "They're talking about a grandson in particular who must be little." The two nodded their heads. "They are telling me that this grandson has told you that he sees them."

The father confirmed that, yes, the kid does say this. "He tells us he's talking to his grandpa." The little boy was telling them this, but they weren't sure whether the boy was actually talking with his grandparents, or if he was hearing from the "wrong side."

I said, "Let me see if I can help you, because the grandparents are doing a lot of talking and they are telling me that they are protectors for the grandchildren. I have no idea what this means, and I'm even hesitant to say it, but they are telling me something about zero. I don't mean a big old circle, I mean the word *zero*. What are they talking about? Do you have any idea?"

They almost fell off their chairs. Apparently, when his grandparents were still alive, the little boy was going trick-or-treating on Halloween. The grandfather had said to him, "Why don't you go out as Zorro?" The little boy didn't know who Zorro was, so the grandfather had told him a number of stories about Zorro saving the day. And they made a costume for this little boy. He went out as Zorro, and that had become the grandfather's pet name for the boy.

"Zorro" and "zero" were close enough that this couple gathered immediately what I was actually hearing. And it was clear that, not only were they hearing from their parents in this moment, but their son was having conversations with them, too!

I can't overemphasize the importance of paying attention and watching for the spirits. They want us to believe in them, to know that they are real and that they are there. If you are skeptical they will still try to reach you, but of course it's going to be harder for them. You just won't be open to the signs they are sending— you'll be setting a high bar and asking them to jump over it.

I did a benefit show for the Boys and Girls Club. There was an older man there with his granddaughter. I was talking with the granddaughter and learned there was a grandson who had died very young. I said to the grandfather, "I know you didn't want to come here today because you don't believe in what I do." He was very nice, and very kind, even as he openly stated that he was a skeptic. But then I started to tell him things about the grandson, and I could see that he was resonating with the things I brought up. Then I told him that the grandson was showing me an animal, a giraffe. The grandfather got all emotional and started crying.

The granddaughter said, "It's in his pocket." And he pulled out of his pocket a little stuffed animal, a giraffe. The granddaughter said that, as they were getting ready to go, he told her that he really didn't believe in anything psychic, but if I mentioned the giraffe then he would know that it was real.

I'm a little nervous telling this story here, to be honest, because it doesn't always work out that I mention the thing that a person intends to be their "sure sign of proof." I don't want to discourage anyone, and I also don't want to encourage people to come to my show with all kinds of things in the pockets and purses—like on the old TV show, *Let's Make A Deal*, when Monty Hall used to say, "I'll give one hundred dollars to the first person who shows me they have a hard-boiled egg in their purse!"

Sometimes it happens—I may mention a piece of jewelry, for example, that the spirit is showing to me and the person I'm reading for will say, "Yes, that's right. I'm wearing my mother's ring," or "Yes, I have my dad's wallet in my pocket." But sometimes I'll be doing a reading and the person they are looking for isn't the one who comes through. It'll be someone else whom the person knows and can confirm, or the one they are looking for comes through with lots of other souls all clamoring to get a word in. While the individual I'm reading can confirm that they know these souls and that their messages are accurate, they might not get the exact confirmation that they tried to set up before coming.

I'm always asked, and I'm grateful to report that yes, the pets we've lost are also safe and sound on the other side. They are not gone forever—every creature created by God goes back to God when it dies. They are all waiting for us, along with the rest of our family members, when we get to the other side, and meanwhile, they are looking out for us.

My friend Debbie had two long-haired dachshunds that she loved with her whole heart, Max and Mimi. Her bond with Mimi surpassed any connection she'd had with any other pets in her life. Debbie would say that she could communicate with Mimi just by looking into her eyes. Mimi just *got* her. Max was the older of her two dogs, but Mimi had gotten sick and had had a large mass removed. Even after the surgery, the prognosis was not good. Before long, Debbie was forced to take Mimi to the emergency hospital in the middle of the night and have her put down. It was the first time she'd ever had to do that with a pet, and it really tore her up. Debbie was devastated; she'd loved that dog completely. She said it was brutal putting her down but knew it was the right thing to do to keep Mimi from suffering. She went home a mess, knowing how sad it would be for Max and for herself to go on after all the years they'd been together.

At the same time, Debbie's dad needed looking after, since he'd just had a triple bypass. So Debbie was really being hit from both sides, worried about her dad and sad about her pet. She prayed that she would get some sort of sign that Mimi was in the light on the other side and okay.

Less than a day after Debbie took Mimi to the hospital, she got an email on her phone. The time stamp said "4:44" and the "From" line said "Mimi." It appeared to be a random advertisement. The subject line said, "Make it Happen!!" Debbie read a little bit of the body of the email, thinking how surreal it was to be thinking of Mimi and to get this email from "Mimi." The email was just an advertisement for closets, so it didn't seem connected, but Debbie had been asking for a sign, so she didn't want to dismiss something that seemed such a strange coincidence. Debbie again took note of the time stamp. She had been working with angel numbers and felt the 4:44 was meaningful. She knew that the number four meant that the angels were with her, so already felt a powerful answer to her prayers for a sign from Mimi. But when she looked up what "444" meant she discovered that it was also a sign that she was where she was supposed to be and that she had the angels' support and guidance on her journey. Knowing that the angels were with her—and specifically her angel dog Mimi— gave Debbie a great deal of comfort. It was exactly what she had been asking for.

Another story involving a beloved pet, and coincidentally another long-haired dachshund, was one I heard from a client who had gone to be with her niece during a painful transition. Her niece's beloved pet, Shaye, had developed a large tumor that had been declared inoperable. The vet advised that it was best to put her to sleep. Both my client and her niece were extremely attached to this dog, as her niece had been living with my client for some time. The two of them had gone together to pick up Shaye when she was a new puppy, and all three had bonded. Shaye loved my client and her niece (and really no one else!) fiercely, and the feelings were mutual. The two decided that they wanted to take her to the family cabin in the mountains for burial. By the time they got there, it was late and dark and quite chilly, so they planned to bury her the next morning. My client burrowed under warm covers to sleep, taking her socks (they were brand new, the first time she'd worn this pair) and laying them on top of the covers in case she had to get up in the middle of the night. The next day, when she went to put on her socks, only one was there. Despite checking all the bedding and under the bed, the missing sock never turned up. Both she and her niece blame a certain dog spirit for absconding with the sock, and they can't help but take it as a playful sign from the other side, since stealing socks was a favorite game of their beloved dog.

Things that are important to you are important to your loved ones on the other side as well. We take our memories with us, nothing is forgotten. At one of my shows, I was reading for a woman whose husband had passed away, and he was the spirit who showed up for her. He mentioned a number of small trinkets of his that he knew she had in what he referred to as "his" drawer in the dresser. She replied that she had just looked through that drawer of stuff that very week. He also said he would be present when her granddaughter got a car, to protect her. And he mentioned a special anniversary that was forthcoming. The woman confirmed that her daughter's twenty-fifth anniversary was coming up in December, and they had just been talking about a party. Then her husband said that he would never forget the snowstorm. The woman confirmed that, on her daughter's wedding day, there had been a major snowstorm. They thought they would have to cancel the whole wedding. Her husband had hired extra people to help shovel the parking lots at the church and at their home, just to get out of the house. They all still talk about that snowstorm to this day. Apparently her husband does, too!

There are many things we can do to connect with a loved one who has crossed. One thing to try is to hold onto some object that belonged to that person when they were living. That object will still contain the energy of the person it belonged to. (Some professional mediums use this tool—called "psychometry"— almost exclusively to connect with their clients' deceased loved ones.) The object could be a piece of clothing or jewelry, a journal, or a pair of glasses. Something that they used over and over while living would be most powerful, but it could literally be anything they once touched.

When my grandmother died, all my older cousins on the Italian side basically ravaged her home for keepsakes. They took everything, from the dishes to the sewing machine. All the furniture, all her little objects. They left nothing; not even a button. Whatever they didn't take home, they got rid of before I had the chance to visit and take a keepsake. The house was being sold, and while it was empty my brother Bobby was asked to house-sit to look after it. I was still feeling a little sorry for myself that I had never got a memento from the home, but I went to see it one last time while Bobby was there, because I thought at least I could take some photos. I had so many memories from that house, and so much history of my father's side of the family had been made there. In fact, the home had been built by my grandparents.

My grandfather had added a second-floor apartment for my uncle and his wife, and that apartment had been the site of many gatherings and parties, a real social hub! You could get to the apartment from the outside, but since so much of the family was always going back and forth between my grandparents' place and my uncle's place, they also had a connecting door on the inside, accessed through my grandparents' bedroom.

As I was taking pictures, I found myself looking at that door, my eyes coming to rest on the old-fashioned glass doorknob.

Suddenly it came to me, and I said, "Bobby! Do you have a screwdriver here?" I realized that every single person, relative or guest, who had ever been there had touched that knob and had left their energy on it. To this day, that humble glass doorknob is more valuable to me than any piece of jewelry or dishes or heirloom furniture. It connects me with my entire family on my father's side.

Maybe this will give you some ideas about the types of things you should consider when you are looking for an object to connect you with your loved one. For one young woman, it was the key her grandmother used to wind her clock every couple of days. For another client, her mother's Bible was a treasured object that she knew contained energy because her mother read it every day. It could be a musical instrument that a loved one played—anything at all. Just give it some thought and you will know where your loved one's energy can be found.

I can't say it often enough—pay close attention for the small signs. It's very unlikely that your loved one will rent a billboard in your neighborhood to send you a message eight feet high. If you are insisting on something flashy, you will likely be disappointed.

I got a letter from a woman in Denver who told me she had read my first book, *Do Dead People Watch You Shower?* She wrote to say how fabulous she thought it was, which I never get tired of hearing. She had bought the book because her father, whom she adored, had passed and she was feeling bereft. Thinking about him and where he was now got her interested in this

Chapter 9: AIR: Always in Reach

subject; she hadn't been before. She told me she was struck by what I had written, that the signs from our deceased loved ones are all around us. She said, "I started to try to relax, and as you instructed, to pay attention to simple things and not take them for granted."

She told me that she was thoroughly a "daddy's girl" and considered her father to be her actual soul mate. I certainly don't mean this in a sexual relationship sense. I understood what she meant—that her father had been a great provider, protector, friend, and confidant. She went on to say that they always played Scrabble together, which she loved. Their games together were so much fun and they had so many great conversations. She told me a story about going to Walmart. "I missed him so much, Concetta, and I was thinking of him as I went about my shopping. When I got back to my car, there, lying on the ground by my car door, was one single Scrabble tile." Remembering how I had said to pay attention to the small things, she bent down to pick it up, knowing with full assurance that it was a sign from her father. It was small, it was simple, it was sweet. It was enough. It meant the world to her.

I think a problem that a lot of folks have here on this side of the veil is that our lives are just so busy, we can't focus. We're all dancing as fast as we can, and I believe that too much multitasking keeps us from quieting ourselves enough to notice our guidance. Prayer can be the most powerful tool for us, but when we are racing in all directions, we can't even quiet our minds enough to pray with clear intention. If you need help from the other side and can possibly manage it, find a way to remove yourself from your daily chaos. Maybe there's a room in your house that's a bit out of the way from the general hubbub. Maybe you can slide into the pew of a church. Maybe you can go for

147

a walk along some body of water—a stream, lake, or the ocean shore. Maybe there is a safe path in the woods nearby, where the only voices you hear are the voices of nature. Take deep breaths. If you are sitting, you may want to close your eyes. Open your heart and your mind. Quietly whisper what is troubling you, and then listen for any response.

You may hear an actual "voice" or thought in reply. This is completely possible, especially if this becomes a regular practice. But please don't hold this as an expectation, certainly not immediately. More likely, you will want to let the other side know what you need, and then be prepared to pay attention. You might try suggesting to the other side something that you will be looking for. But try not to make it a demand, like a "giraffe in a pocket." Be open to noticing anything that could symbolize your loved one's intention.

Chapter 10

Sex, Ghosts, and Haunted Houses

I got a text from a client one day who was horrified because she thought she had been attacked in her sleep.

"I'm at a bed and breakfast with my family and I woke up in the middle of the night and saw a figure next to my bed!" She wrote. "It was holding me down and I couldn't move. Call me ASAP."

I called her and found out she was staying in a very haunted place that dated back to the Civil War. The home had also been a stop on the Underground Railroad. This place wasn't just *haunted*, it was *totally freaking haunted*!

"In my experience, I've come across some energies who, for one reason or another, often because of fear, don't choose to be with God by going into the light, so they stay stuck and cause trouble," I said when we chatted on the phone. "You need to protect yourself before you go to sleep; imagine white light all around you. Also, there's a reason people say their prayers before bed. It literally clears the room of negative energy."

"This ghost was so scary," she said. "I tried to scream and couldn't make a sound, and I tried to move and this thing was physically pinning me down! Is that even possible?"

"Yes, it is," I said. "If that ever happens again, you just have to say, 'In the name of God, you must *go*!' Because a spirit that isn't in the light will leave right away when you bring in the big guns."

I know this works because I've actually had to protect myself from getting sexually attacked by a ghost.

Eww, right? Let me explain...

When I was sleeping one night, I became aware of a really foul smell and felt like something heavy was on top of me. I sensed anger and aggression. Then, all of a sudden, I realized that whatever this thing was, it was trying to be intimate with me. I tried to push it off me, and I felt a cold, mean energy as something gripped both of my wrists and held them down.

What the heck is happening here? I've experienced that thing where you are having a bad dream and your body feels paralyzed and you can't seem to wake up. This was not that.

I couldn't scream, I couldn't move. It was terrifying. That's when I knew this was an energy that was not in the light and it was trying to get busy, if you know what I'm talking about. I looked next to me and saw John sound asleep, totally unaware that this was happening. Since I couldn't speak, I knew I had to *think* of my prayers to get this energy off of me. (Always remember this: Your thoughts are just as powerful as your words.) So I visualized myself making the sign of the cross and I said to myself, "In the name of God, *go!*" My intention was strong, and before I could even finish the thought—*poof*—this thing was gone.

So yes, there are dark energies that, unfortunately, really want to take you down. But, at the opposite end of the spectrum, there are spirits who come into your space to make you feel loved, and that can be a very intimate experience.

John and I had only been married about two years, and we were living in an old Colonial-style house that he had renovated in West Orange, New Jersey. He'd redone the kitchen and bathrooms, and had turned an old attic into a master bedroom suite. I was sleeping one night with John next to me, and I woke up in the middle of the night to the sensation that I was having sex. I knew it wasn't John because we only have sex when we are awake! (And, at the time, we were trying to get me pregnant, so there was a *lot* of sex to be had.) But this was different. I felt the pressure of someone on top of me, and every other sensation you feel when you're being intimate. I felt love, tenderness, gentleness, but I knew this was not John.

Am I being kissed by a ghost?

At first I was a little freaked-out, but this ghost was so sweet and so loving and gentle. There was so much love in whatever was happening that I really thought it was a dream. My conscious mind said, "You'd better wake up for this one!"

Is it wrong that I'm enjoying this?

I finally woke up and I couldn't see a face. I just felt the pressure of someone—a male energy—on top of me and caressing me very tenderly. I realized it wasn't necessarily the act that was so incredible; it was the *love* that came over me during the act. It was euphoric in a way that just wasn't human. It was that feeling when you're so in love you don't care if they kiss you, hold your hand, or hand you a ballpoint pen, you just want to be in their presence. If I had to describe it in just a couple of words, I'd say the feeling was like an "intense *kindness*."

Who is this? They feel so familiar...

I figured that I must have known this spirit in another lifetime. There is no way I could have felt so engulfed in bliss without having been this spirit's lover in a past life. Whether I was his wife, or girlfriend, or both, this ghost was no stranger to me. I never would have believed it was possible had I not experienced it for myself. When I tried to focus on a face or maybe get an impression of his name, this energy just sort of lifted up and I could no longer feel it on me.

I don't know who you are, but if you're not busy tomorrow, could you please come back?

That's not really cheating, is it?

I never forgot that encounter. As I've had time to process it all, I think the mysterious Casanova came to me so that I could feel how a deep love between souls truly never dies, even when we travel over different lifetimes—a truly *eternal* love. It also helped me counsel my clients. I've had many people who have told me similar stories, where they wonder if they're dreaming that their loved one was in bed with them—they felt so cared for and safe while they're sleeping, complete with kissing and all the rest of it.

I tell these clients that, whether they were married for two minutes, twenty years, or not married at all, a spirit might make their presence known in the bedroom. I now know that love can be transferred to us in very intimate ways while we are sleeping.

One story I'll never forget came from a lady who had lost her husband of nearly fifty years.

"I'm useless without him," she said, her heart heavy with grief, when she sat down in my office.

Immediately, I saw a man next to her from the other side. He said he was her husband, and he talked about their wedding song.

"Our wedding anniversary would have been next week," she said, wiping a tear.

"He's saying to tell you that it wasn't your imagination, and that you weren't dreaming. Do you know what he's talking about?" I asked.

She shared that when it was her birthday recently, all day, she was so sad that he wasn't with her to celebrate.

"When I went to bed that night, I was so upset," she said. "In the middle of the night, I woke up and felt someone lying next to me in bed. I got this feeling it was my husband, and that he was holding my hand."

She said they had been married so long that they were at a point where sex was not important anymore.

"But just to have him there and have him hold me again felt as good as it did when I first met him in my twenties," she said. "I so wanted to believe that it was him. So when I came to this reading, I said, 'If you were really visiting me, honey, please tell me so through Concetta.' And now that you said all this, I know it was true."

One of the craziest ghost stories I've heard was not from one of my clients. It was something I read on the *New York Post*'s infamous Page Six, where I myself have appeared a couple of times. It was a story about a thirty-year-old woman from England who says she's had sex with at least twenty ghosts, and now...wait for it...she's engaged to a poltergeist. I'm not sure this was a wise move, as poltergeists are notoriously destructive. I have too many tchotchkes and other breakables in my home to get involved with one of those, but she seems smitten. I had to laugh when I read her saying, "There was no going down on one knee—he doesn't have knees..."

Well, right.

She describes her lover as an "incredible energy" and mentions being able to hear his voice, describing it as "deep, sexy, and real." I giggled again (or maybe I rolled my eyes) when she confessed to "doing it" in the bathroom of the airplane on the way home from Australia, where she'd met the spirit, making the two of them members of the Metaphysical Mile-High Club.

She did not describe any of the kind of crazy activity I associate with a poltergeist, and I hope for her sake he's a quiet one. She does say that her orgasms with this spirit were way better than what she'd had with her previous (still in human form) fiancé!

Needless to say, not every ghost story is quite so sexy. Most hauntings—whether benign or hostile—are spirits who are attached in some way to a place and are unable to successfully cross to the other side, for whatever reason.

I've talked a lot about my travels with John and our friends, and I know I've mentioned our visit to Rothenburg, Germany. Rothenburg is a walled city. Cars are not permitted, so we had to park our rental outside the walls (which are very cool and covered in vines, with fruit trees growing on top of them—there are stairs you can climb to walk around a portion of the wall). We had arrangements to stay at this beautiful bed-and-breakfast that had been remodeled. Our accommodations were so fantastic, it was like stepping back centuries in time. The four-poster bed was very unusual. You climbed down into it, like into a crate, rather than climbing up onto a mattress. The bathroom was enormous; likely it had not originally been a bathroom. It had beautiful, sparkling white tile and a very tiny window. But what a view from that window! You could see a sweeping vista of half the city, all the rooftops and some of the cobblestone streets. Gazing out, I had a strong sense memory that I had lived there before. It felt so familiar.

But, during the night I woke up to the sound of children laughing and playing, and I heard footsteps outside our room. The next morning I asked the housekeeper how many kids the proprietors had, as I'd heard them the night before. The owners were two gay men, and I was told they didn't have any children. Nor were there any children presently staying at the B and B. I kept hearing them, however, and one night during our stay, I felt someone tickle my feet! I'd gotten warm in bed, so had put my feet outside the bedcovers, and I felt the gentle, very sweet tickle on my feet, along with more laughter. I have to assume this was kids in spirit, and—given how old the city was, and knowing how in bygone times there was even more likelihood for a person to die very young—I imagine that these kids may have crossed a very long time ago.

All my life, I've known of the existence of spirits side by side with us in the flesh. And all my life I've had experiences and encounters, knowing they were there. Mostly I've experienced this by hearing. Not until I was an adult did I experience anything physical. It was probably a good thing to not have this kind of experience before I was mature enough to understand. But I always knew the spirits were there. Their hugs and kisses come through.

When my mother passed away, I was devastated. So many times thereafter I've felt her presence walk up to my bed. Or, I should say, "glide" up to my bed, or "fly" up to my bed, and I've felt her warm embrace. I've felt her hand caress my face. There is no question in my mind that the spirits are very capable of expressing their love physically, through energy like I felt from my mother and many other dear souls.

So, before you doze off, you may want to put a dab of your favorite perfume behind your ear in case you have a late-night visit from your late husband—or even a former partner from another century! If it's a love-fest with your loved one, enjoy the reminder that unconditional love is everywhere when you're in the light, and all you have to do is receive the gift with open arms.

I was working on this chapter around Halloween week, so everywhere I looked, I was seeing ghosts—not just in my own home, which is pretty much par for the course, but all over the place, in every store window and front yard. Of course these were mostly of the cartoon variety, cardboard cutouts or blow-ups, or bits of cloth hanging from a wire. It made me curious about how many people have actually seen a ghost in real life. I did a little searching on the internet, and it seems that only about 20 percent of people in various polls say they have seen a ghost. But there didn't seem to be any polls about how many have *heard* a ghost, or smelled one, or seen things move around due to a spirit's influence. I would be willing to bet there are a lot of folks who have experienced these types of things who have simply decided that there must be a logical explanation for what they've experienced and have simply talked themselves out of what really happened. Even people in my close circle resist the most logical explanation of what their eyes, ears, and other senses are telling them—that they are in the presence of a ghost!

When my friend Mushy turned sixty, we wanted to make a big deal of her milestone birthday. I said, "Mush, what would you like? Is there something special you want? Would you like a big party, or maybe to do something special?" Mushy replied that she had never in her life been to Europe. She'd been to Mexico with me when I was doing shows there, but her husband didn't really like to travel, so they hadn't really gotten around the world as much as John and I had. So she decided she'd like to see Italy. I was totally on board for that. I would go back to Italy any time, for any reason. It's so beautiful and has so much history—and the *food! Mamma mia!*

As we started to plan the trip, our friend Debbie said she wanted to go, too, so the three of us headed off, just us girls.

In Rome, a city I've visited before and could never get tired of, we rented an amazing duplex apartment on the Pantheon square, with bedrooms and a bathroom upstairs and a kitchen and living area downstairs; it even had a washer and dryer. It truly doesn't get any better than that. We took in the Coliseum and the Spanish Steps. And. We. Shopped.

The most beautiful things in the world are made in Rome— jewelry, pocketbooks, clothes—everywhere you look you see something stylish or artistic. Debbie and I went crazy. What was Mushy interested in? She found a store that sold iPhone covers made in China. Seriously, with everything in the city to choose from, this is what she homed in on? She bought a few of these, but long after we had left that shop, she was still thinking about them. Her granddaughters all have phones, and she kept thinking she should have gotten more iPhone covers for them. Debbie and I thought she was nuts, but, hey, this was her birthday expedition and whatever made her happy, we were game for. After a while obsessing, she decided she wanted to go back to that store, but we couldn't find it. We walked up and down and around and round, wasting hours of our Roman holiday on a shop with "Made in China" iPhone covers. And the biggest irony was that, once we were back in New Jersey and she put the covers on actual phones, there was something about them that actually prevented the phone from working properly. All that drama for these things that didn't even work. Debbie and I cracked up.

But back to our Italian adventure, Mushy wanted to take the double-decker tourist bus around the city, and so we did. It was one of those where you pay for the bus once but can get off or on at various points to get a closer look at the attractions or shops. We kept asking Mushy if she wanted to get off to see various sights, but she never did. She just enjoyed sitting on the top of the bus, viewing everything. She had a great time, and that's all that mattered to us.

On Sunday, Debbie and I wanted to go to church, but it was near the end of our stay, and Mushy—being the good German that she is—wanted to tidy up her things before going home. She decided to stay at the apartment and do *laundry*, which Debbie and I couldn't help laughing about. I have to digress once more here. We have a wonderful girlfriend group in New Jersey, called the PPP. I can't say what the initials stand for or the other girls would feed me to the fishes. Once we all decided to go to the Jersey Shore and rent a couple of hotel rooms. The weather wasn't super-hot, as it was September; summer was over, but it was still nice enough for the beach. We all took the bare minimum, except for Mushy. She made ten trips to her car for bags, chips, groceries, bottles of vodka—she could have stayed for a month and not have had to go shopping. Mushy is always over-prepared and over-the-top. Even when making dinner for friends, she could use the food she'd prepared for a banquet. She always makes enough for two hundred people. We all laugh and bring containers because we know there is going to be food to take home. We make fun of her mercilessly, but we love her to death and she knows it.

Debbie and I had originally only planned to visit the church, which is just out-and-out gorgeous. But once we got there, we ended up staying for Mass and wandered around for a while afterward. We got back to the apartment a good bit later than we had planned, and Mushy was waiting for us.

"Why did you come back and then go back out without asking me if I wanted to go with you?" was the first thing out of her mouth. We had no idea what she was talking about. "I was in the shower while the laundry was running and I heard youse come upstairs—I heard you laughing. But then you left before I got out of the shower."

Debbie and I looked at each other and Debbie said, very solemnly, "Cornelia," (that's Mushy's real name), "we never came back till just now. I don't know what you heard, but I promise you, it wasn't us." Mushy was beside herself. She said, "I *definitely* heard someone come in, come upstairs. And I heard *laughing. Someone* was in the bedroom, outside the bathroom door. This is totally freaking me out." She then explained how, when she went to take her shower, she didn't know how to lock the downstairs door—it had a funny kind of a latch—so she just put the chain on. When she came down from her shower, after hearing someone come in, she saw that the chain was still on the door. She couldn't figure out how we'd come in and gone out, getting in with the chain on the door, then somehow fastening it again after we left. It seemed impossible, yet she had been sure it was us.

I had to bite my tongue. Mushy was already upset. I didn't want to put gasoline on the fire by suggesting there had been some dead people watching her shower!

On a trip to Ireland, John and I visited Blarney Castle—yes, the one with the stone that is supposed to give anyone kissing it the gift of gab. I have a fear of heights, so there was no frickin' way that I was going to climb up there, bend over backward, and kiss that stone. And, frankly, I'm pretty sure that nobody would suggest that I *needed* to kiss that stone. I think I'm already notorious for my gift of gab. But John wanted to go up and tour the castle, so I said this was fine and I'd just keep my feet on the ground and wander around the gardens.

I must tell you that the gardens at Blarney Castle were as green as green could be. I know Ireland is notorious for being green, but this was truly much more vivid than anywhere I'd been in my life. What stood out for me were the hydrangea bushes. They seemed to flourish there in that climate. In the mountains in New Jersey, where I live, I have planted hydrangeas, but they are so temperamental. They never seem to do well, and I only ever get a couple of flowers on them. I'm actually thinking of just taking them out because they always disappoint me. But in the castle gardens, the hydrangeas were covered in lush blooms. And such an unusual color, they almost looked "antique" to me. They weren't a bright blue or bright pink but a more muted combination of both blue and pink, really the most beautiful color.

As I walked, I could not help admiring the castle, even if I was only taking in its exterior. But at one point I saw someone waving to me from a second-floor window and, while I could not actually see the person, I assumed it was John and waved back.

After a while, John rejoined me outside. Just to confirm my assumption, I said, "So, was that you waving to me from the second floor?"

He said, "No, I wasn't on the second floor. I didn't wave to you."

I said, "Huh. I wonder who that was? I saw someone waving to me while I was walking in the garden."

John said, "Well, it couldn't have been someone on the second floor, because that floor is closed."

I said, "It was definitely the second floor," and John said, "Well, I don't see how. I just took the tour, and that part of the castle is closed. You can't go in."

Needless to say, I found this strange, so when we saw a tour guide, I asked him, "My husband said that the second floor of the castle is closed. Can you tell me why that is?"

He said, rather strangely, "I don't have an answer that I can give you."

I wasn't sure what that meant. I said, "Well, I saw *someone* on that floor—they waved to me." He just smiled.

John and I have taken a number of cruises together over the years, but we took a different sort of cruise in England with

another couple—a two-week tour on a canal boat. That is, a
haunted canal boat.

These boats are very small, with a little galley, a little salon, two
bedrooms that are meant to sleep two people in a large "twin"
bed, and a small bunk area that is meant for a child to sleep in.
The two-adults-in-a-large twin was not working out at all for
me, so I was using the kid's bunk to sleep in, leaving the slightly
larger bed to John. The small child's area had a shelf opposite the
bed, and I stowed my luggage and clothes there. When they talk
about "ship shape" meaning neat, you soon understand why it's
necessary. There just isn't any room for a mess!

Even though the quarters were tight, I felt very comfortable in
this little bunk. And very cared for, too. Each night when I'd turn
in, I could feel someone pull the covers up around me, tucking
me in. With my background, this wasn't something I found
upsetting—really, it was just sweet and comforting to me.

The canal we were traveling was a narrow waterway with woods
on both sides. From time to time, the boat would dock and we'd
get off to explore one of the towns along the way. At Stratford,
for instance, we walked up a little path from the canal onto the
cobbled streets to visit tiny shops. There was also an outdoor
market selling fruits and vegetables and lots of local handmade
things, like dresses and sweaters, potholders, and doilies. All
these towns also seemed to have phenomenal bakeries. My
favorite treat was meringue. It's virtually all egg white and sugar,
but at different places they would make it in different shapes and
all different sizes. Terrible for me, but I love it.

One day we were docked and were on shore, checking out the
attractions and shops. After a meal, we returned to the boat to

sleep. As I mentioned, I had all my clothes stowed on the small shelves across from the bed, but when I got to my little area, I saw my nightgown on the bed, folded perfectly. But even better was what happened the next morning. After I woke up, I got dressed and went out to the galley to have breakfast with John and our friends. When I came in, John said off-handedly, "Why'd you get out of bed with me last night?"

I asked, "What do you mean?"

He said, "Well, you were in bed with me and then at one point, you got up and left."

I said, "No I didn't, John. I was sleeping where I was before, in the kid's bed."

He was adamant, saying, "Come on, Concetta. I know you were in bed with me at first. I felt you next to me. I could feel you spooning me."

I said, "I hate to break it to you, sweetheart, but I was not in bed with you. I think that must have been a ghost."

John has come a long way over the years with me, from skeptic to "almost believer," but this was too much for him. He got all flustered and said, "Oh okay, I guess I must have been dreaming." I had to laugh.

You may never have experienced anything as dramatic as these stories, but sometimes the dead folks are literally just passing through. Recently I was in Florida, sleeping in a hotel. In the middle of the night, I felt someone on top of me, with pressure on my shoulder as if someone was trying to get me to turn over.

I was alone in bed, so I knew it was a spirit. This was at an ordinary beach hotel, not especially haunted, but then, a spirit can be anywhere they have some connection to. The feeling did not last long before they were on their way. I said a prayer, "Be with God," both to benefit this soul and to protect myself.

In all honesty, I don't know why certain spirits opt to visit in this way. Is it karmic? Is it simply opportunity? My best guess is that the loving spirits are ones we have known and who care for us, even if we were not in an exclusive loving relationship with them on this side. Maybe in a past lifetime we were. The times we need to be able to protect ourselves are whenever we encounter a heavy, dark, negative-energy spirit. If you ever have this type of experience, just remember that God said, "He who asks in my name shall receive." So, if you need help getting rid of an unwanted visitor, you need to give God a shout.

I have one more story to tell about being kissed by a ghost, and this one is very important to me. Shortly before I was to do my first-ever public show, my father crossed to the other side. Of course I missed him terribly, but he came to me right away to let me know that he was with my brother Harold, so I knew all was well with him. He kissed me very gently on the lips. For me the feeling was simply miraculous, and I am so grateful to have had this experience.

Then, just a few weeks after that, at my first show, I could feel my father's presence so strongly. I can barely describe just how strongly his presence permeated the room. It was overwhelming. I could feel all the love he had for me just enveloping me in the embrace of his energy.

But later, in the car going home, it was Mushy who turned to me and said, "Concetta. Pop was there. Did you feel him?" She was simply beaming. Mushy has been my longest-term and best friend, since we were little girls. I've always been able to confide in her regarding my spiritual experiences. But she herself has never been at all spiritually oriented. Just not her thing. It was amazing to me to see her so spiritually lifted, enlightened, and touched that way. The light was all around her; she was just touched with joy. I want everyone to know that this kind of experience is truly possible for anyone, whether they believe they are spiritual or not. The love and grace from the other side touches us all.

Chapter 11

Believe It or Not

Very surprisingly, there are still skeptics in this world when it comes to psychic ability. Shocking, right? Well, God love 'em. My own husband was one, and I love him dearly, so I've had long practice being at peace about this. I always say that I don't mind anyone having their doubts, but I appreciate it when a doubting Thomas will at least keep an open mind. I've changed many minds in the time I've been doing this work. I stand by my ability and I promise you 100 percent that, if I tell you I've heard something, seen something, smelled something, or felt something, then I've heard it, seen it, smelled, or felt it. I'm not reading anyone's mind; it's the spirits showing me everything. Without them, I wouldn't have a clue.

Frankly, *with* them, I don't have a clue. I love to say (it always gets a laugh) that I don't know what I'm talking about, and that's the truth. The only thing I can tell you is that when I hear something, I'm sure. It is very frustrating when someone I'm doing a reading for tells me they can't validate something that I've told them, but I still know it's true. I'll say, "Write it down," "Ask your wife," or, "Ask your mother." Someone in the family is going to know what I'm talking about, even if I don't! I cannot tell you how many times a client has left me, shaking their head or racking their brain, only to call me or write me a short time later to say, "You. Were. Right."

I did a reading for one of the hosts on a radio show in Chicago. I told her that her mother was showing me some kind of linens that she would recognize. Right away, the host told me that her mother used to do embroidery, and she had one of her mother's linen pieces with the image of a cross on her bedside table. But there were other things I mentioned, like that her mother was showing her the number three, and she wasn't sure what that meant. So even though I knew she wanted to believe what I was saying, there was likely a little doubt. I get that. If you can't confirm something, then how can you really be sure? Later I got an email from her saying that, while we were on the air, her sister was listening and going nuts because she had been seeing the number three all the time. It's not a perfect science, I knew her mother was showing me the number three, but I did not know that this was aimed at her other daughter, the host's sister! I think you get the picture and can understand why I hope folks will keep their minds open, if and when they have a reading, and share any information they are given that they don't understand in the moment.

At one of my big shows, I was doing a reading for a woman in the audience who was sitting with a younger woman. The younger woman had a look on her face like she wasn't quite sure all of this was real. In the course of the reading, I learned that the younger woman was the daughter of the woman I was reading for. In any case, as soon as I went up to the first woman, her husband came through right away. He kept talking about their life together, and she was validating the recollections I was able to share with her. But then he told me that he had died on a special occasion. At first I thought he was referring to his wedding anniversary, and I said to her, "Did your husband cross on your wedding anniversary? Why am I seeing the symbol for a wedding?"

And she said, "He died at my daughter's wedding." I felt so bad to have brought this up! Then she said that her daughter had felt terrible about it because her father had died on the day she got married.

But then the man said, *"Show her this."* And I saw doves, white doves, which I conveyed to the mother and daughter. It turns out that they had turned loose white doves at the wedding celebration. At this, the daughter started to cry.

She came up to me after the show and said, "Now I know that my father is in heaven, and that he's okay, because you would never have known about the doves. That tells me he's really here with us." That made me very happy, to have been able to convince her that "dead" is not dead, and that our loved ones are with us always.

At the same show, I spoke with a skeptical older gentleman sitting right in the front row. As soon as I started to talk to him, I knew his wife had crossed. She was showing me a vase—it sparkled with glitter or something. When I described it, he was shocked. He told me it was the last gift he had given her, and that she had picked the vase out for herself. He wanted to get her jewelry, but she had told him she really wanted the vase. I also mentioned to him that she was standing with three people she wanted me to know were very important to him. It turned out that, in the last six months before she'd died, he'd had three other great losses. One was a very dear friend of hers, one was a dear cousin of theirs, and sadly, one was a mother of theirs. He wept uncontrollably, but was extremely grateful. He came up to me at the book signing after the event to say how much the night had meant to him. He had been on the fence about coming at all, but felt strongly that, if there were anything he heard that he could verify, he would know that I was the real deal. More importantly, he'd know that his loved ones were still around him. He was extremely grateful. He wanted to give me a gift. He had an expensive pen in his pocket that he offered to me, but I would not accept it. Instead, I asked him to remember that his wife had told him that she remembered all the beautiful things he used to write to her in the cards he gave her. And again he started crying. It was very sweet, very emotional.

When I hear the spirits tell me something, I know I can rely on it. It could be something quite ordinary, but the fact that they are able to accurately convey memories, describe situations or events, or, in some cases, predict what will happen at some point to come is what makes it extraordinary to us here.

When I do readings at a big show, I will usually cut to the chase and ask people whom they are hoping to hear from, because I want to be able to get to as many as possible in the short time we're all together. But when I do a reading in my office, we have more time, so I often just let things unfold with whoever shows up, unless the client specifically asks to hear from a particular person. Recently I did a reading for a woman whose father had passed, but she had said that he was not who she had hoped to hear from. I said to her, "There's a man standing next to you, and I can't tell who he is to you. I only know that's who you are looking for."

She said, "Yes, that's true." Apparently it was a sad situation where this individual had taken his own life. It wasn't a love interest; my client was happily married. But she was thrilled to hear from this man (I'll call him "Joe"), and told me she was very close to his family. Joe gave her a lot of information that was personal, some she could validate and some she said she would have to look into, as others might know more about certain things than she did.

Joe wanted me to tell her that he was with the dog. My client explained that, after Joe died, the family dog died, too. Joe had adored the dog. They'd had a real bond, and family members had said that the dog had probably died because he missed Joe. I told my client that Joe said the family was getting another dog. But there was something specific he was trying to say about the old dog and the new dog that I couldn't understand.

My client had no clue about another dog—she hadn't heard anything about it. But after she left my office, she called Joe's wife to tell her about the reading. The wife told her that she had gotten a call from the people their dog had originally come from. The mother of that dog had another litter, and they were going to be getting another puppy from the mother of the original dog. She was freaking out because she realized that's what Joe had been trying to tell her. The whole thing brought her a lot of happiness because the family had another dog they could give love to like the one they missed, and they also knew that Joe was close by, keeping tabs on all the people he cared about and the pets in their lives.

A woman came to me—I knew her husband had died because he came through right away. He kept saying something about a wedding. He told me, and she confirmed, that he had died at his own son's wedding. It was very sad. He told me that there was a photograph taken of the three of them—him, his wife, and their son. She said, no, there really was no such photo that she was aware of. He went on to give a mountain of information about a dog they'd had when they were young that they'd loved very much. It had been a rescue dog and had been hit by a car. He was happy to tell her that the dog was there with him, and that made her happy, too. And that was that.

Maybe a week after her reading, the woman called me. She wanted to let me know that an old friend of the family had sent her a letter and in it was a photo of her, her deceased husband,

and their son, taken on the son's wedding day. The letter her friend had sent said that she'd been going through some old things and had come across a picture they had taken that day, and thought she would want to have it.

A lovely girl came to my house. She was young—in her thirties, I guess—and she was very upset. Her grandmother had died, and she wanted desperately to hear from her. Apparently, her grandmother had raised her because her own mother had a drug addiction. She was happy when her grandmother came through and told her many things that she was able to validate. One thing she mentioned, or rather she showed to me, were these really sweet cups that my client had taken out of her grandmother's house. There wasn't a lot of stuff, but there were these teacups. The grandmother was saying to me that the granddaughter had the tea set. And the young woman said to me, "No, that's not right. I don't have the tea set, just the tea cups." So I got that wrong, right?

Nope.

A short time later, my client got back in touch. It turned out that there was a relative who lived somewhere else, and they had the other pieces of the set. Lo and behold, the relative had called this girl and said, "We want to know if you'd like to have the rest of the set. It's only fair—we know that you loved your grandmother and we know you have the cups, but you'd probably love to have the whole set."

Here's another one that happened very recently...

Only a couple weeks ago, as I was working on this book, I had a client come to me to hear from her mother who had passed away.

During the reading, I smelled the fragrance Evening in Paris, and she confirmed, "Oh yes, that's what my mother wore."

I said, "Your mother is showing me the bottle and saying that you have it."

She said, "No, I don't have the bottle, but that is the perfume my mother always wore." I mentioned some other things, including a beautiful necklace that came from Paris, which she had gotten from one of her relatives, and she validated that. But the great thing was that, about a week later, the woman called and told me that her sister, who lives in California, had come to visit her.

She said, "Oh I have something for you," and went to her suitcase, coming back with an Evening in Paris perfume bottle. She said, "I got it at a flea market. When I saw it, I thought it might remind you of Mommy." My client was completely blown away, since she had never told her sister about the reading and what her mother had said about the bottle.

I never like giving anyone bad news, but if there is something I feel they need to know, I don't want to withhold helpful information. I will always be careful about how I word things if I need to offer a warning, and cushion any less-than-ideal news as best I can. One such situation was with a doctor who had come to me for a reading. There was nothing in particular on his radar, no special reason he had come. I believe he just wanted to see what would happen, and who might come through.

There were a number of messages he could validate, but one thing I heard, and told him, was that his son was not well, and that he would be diagnosed with something. I didn't know what it was—I was just reporting what I had heard from the spirits.

But I also heard that eventually his son would be all right, and I let him know this, too. The doctor got a little ruffled, not very happy with that message because, he told me, his son was fine. But he left somewhat satisfied, taking all the *other* information that he *was* happy with.

A good while later, he called my assistant Elena to make another appointment. He wanted to tell her that I'd been right. His son had gotten very, very ill and they didn't know what was wrong with him. The boy was finally diagnosed with Lyme disease and it took a long time for him to get well. He had gone through some kind of light therapy and was doing much better. I know it wasn't easy to hear that there was a problem, but I hope he was comforted while they were all going through his son's illness by knowing the other side had said all would be well in the end.

One of my favorite "I told you so" stories is from a good friend I first met when she came to me as a client. We only got to be friends over time. She was a lawyer, and while she was good at her job and loved it, her real dream was to become a judge.

In our reading, her father came through, and he showed me the judge's robes and said that this would happen. I was very happy to tell her that she would get her wish. Yes, she would be a judge.

Well, as I may have mentioned before, the other side is not great about predicting timing. Their sense of time is eternal—on the other side there really is no "time" as we know it here. Sometimes I will get indications of a time of year or a particular month or date. They might show me a number or a letter to indicate a month, or maybe something that symbolizes a season. But as far as an exact date, I've never yet found a reliable means to predict. So, for a year my friend was anticipating news of her promotion, but it didn't happen. In the second year, she was anticipating it, and it didn't happen. In the third year, she was no longer anticipating it, so maybe she was less disappointed than she'd been the first two years. In the fourth year, she decided the wait was really too long and she was now seriously doubting it would happen. In the fifth year, she said to me, "You're a nice lady, Concetta, and I think what you do helps people. But I think you are wrong on this one."

I said to her, "I'm so sorry, because timing is something that I cannot predict. But I stand by what I heard and saw."

She said, "Well, I love ya anyway."

In the seventh year, she became Judge Suzy Q. Smith. (I've changed her name here to avoid being found guilty and thrown in the slammer for contempt of court!) I must say I could not have been more pleased to prove that the judge had misjudged. But I can't take the credit—her father had told me it would happen, so I knew it would.

Besides someone I'm reading for not being able to confirm information until later, I also love the moments I call "deer in the headlights." There's something about a psychic medium telling you what a dead loved one is saying that just stuns people. It really isn't a thing that happens every day for most people, and so, even when they *want* to hear the messages (that's what they came for, after all), they sometimes can't absorb them or make sense of them. One that makes me laugh every time I think about it is when I was reading for a woman and I told her about a bar where she and her friends hung out when they were younger. I said to her, "He's saying the name, 'Mike.' Can you tell me who that is?" and she shook her head, looking puzzled, like she hadn't got a clue.

She said, "No, no, I don't know."

And her girlfriend next to her jabbed her with her elbow and said, "That's your *husband*, stupid!"

In another case, I got a letter from a woman who had attended one of my shows last year. I had mentioned at the show that I love to hear about things that someone can't make sense of in the moment but later figures out. In her letter, the woman told me that her husband had come through and was saying something about living by the water. She shook her head, not understanding what he meant. Later that day, in a calmer state of mind, she realized that they had lived by the water together *three separate times*. They'd had, she said, three homes, right next to the water. And yet, when she was getting the reading, this did not compute!

Sometimes even *I* doubt what I'm hearing, even though I should know better. A woman came to see me at my office. Her husband had had a heart attack at home and, quick as lightning, he was gone. When I asked for him, he came through right away. He told me that today was their wedding anniversary, which she confirmed, and he showed me that the two of them had gotten tattoos. She said, "Yes, we got matching tattoos." And then he told me that she had gotten clothes from him recently. I thought that couldn't be right. How would he have given her clothes when he was already on the other side? With a little trepidation, I repeated to his wife what he had told me.

To my surprise, she said, "Concetta, it's so funny. He passed away a year ago. I finally moved and got rid of all his clothes and everything." She said in her smaller home it was just too difficult to keep the things. But afterward, she was sorry she hadn't kept anything.

Lo and behold, the dry cleaners called her—a year after his death—to tell her they still had clothes her husband had dropped off. She was blown away by this—and so was I.

Chapter 12

The Proof Is in the Nanny Cam

My head is spinning. Is yours? Can you believe how much technology has changed our lives in just the last couple of decades? Forget decades, even, how about the last few years? Yes, this is our reality show, and we can post all of it on our very own YouTube channel.

Some of this stuff has been coming for a long time. Back in elementary school, we used to get a newsletter called *The Weekly Reader*. It was full of articles that young children would find interesting. One story I remember clearly was about how, in the future, we would have something like a TV screen so we could see each other when we were talking on the phone. When I was eight, this seemed like a very fun and exciting thing. Now I'm in my sixties and we've got it, and strangely, it's not all that fun and exciting. Have you ever accidentally butt-dialed someone before you were out of your pajamas and discovered that you also accidentally hit "Facetime"? Yikes!

As I've mentioned numerous times before, the dead are great with tech. Maybe once I'm on the other side I'll understand it, too. One can only hope. But tech has given them more ways to tell us they are around and looking after us. A good number of my clients have told me about phone calls they've received from the beyond. There's no other way to explain a call coming from a loved one's old uncharged cell phone after that person has passed. The way things are going, John may have the last laugh. I may *actually* be taking calls from the top floor; the phone lines are definitely open.

Of course everyone is on the computer now, and that gives the spirits a lot more ways to connect than in past generations. Again, I have no idea how this works, other than I know they are able to manipulate energy, which means anything to do with electricity. Do they need to know your password to hack your Facebook account? I doubt it.

A gentleman came to see me after his wife died. He told me that he felt his wife was sending him small messages through his computer. Apparently he was very knowledgeable about computers and could think of no "rational" explanation for what he was experiencing. It was nothing big, just certain icons would show up that were meaningful to him, or certain pop-ups that reminded him of her. He said that there was simply no explanation he could think of for why these signs would be happening. One was an ad for a movie that they had really liked. It wasn't even a current film, and it happened more than once. Another time, he was going to visit his daughter, who was in college in Florida, and again something popped up that had to do with the very town in Florida he was going to. He was something of an expert, and he explained that he was sure it didn't have to do with cookies that had noticed preferences of his, but rather, these things seemed to come very spontaneously if he was doing something or thinking about something related to him or his wife, or their family. He was totally convinced that his wife was talking to him through his computer. And I'm pretty sure he was right.

Our cameras are picking up some pretty interesting things, too. I have a client whose daughter was very sick. As the girl lay in her hospital bed, my client and her husband took photos of her and were astonished to see orbs of light flying all around her in the pictures. They decided to take a video and, even more amazingly, the orbs appeared to fly by her face as the sleeping child began to smile. They seemed to be caressing her face and body. When she was awake, the girl told her family that a nice lady had come to see her, and she described a great-grandmother (whom she'd never met) to a T. She said the lady told her everything was going to be all right. Sure enough, the little girl recovered. Her parents believe that the orbs were somehow the great-grandmother in spirit form, and I agree.

This is far from the only time I've heard a story like this. In a previous reading I'd done for a woman, she told me that her daughter was having trouble conceiving. I'd told her that she would ultimately be successful. Well, it took her five years and trying a number of things, but she was finally successful with in-vitro fertilization. So in this new reading, I said to her that the spirits on the other side were showing signs that they know the new baby, and that the baby knows them. At that, she pulled out her iPhone and showed me pictures she had taken of the baby in her crib, with these orbs floating all around her.

Social media has brought us closer in many ways. We post our children's milestones, our accomplishments, and our vacation photos, or sometimes sadder things, like news of a beloved pet's passing. I see some people getting braver, too, about what they share of their life experiences. It gives me hope that we are getting to a place of greater understanding. The other day I saw on Twitter: "The baby keeps looking just over my shoulder and smiling, so that means we have ghosts, right?" You bet it does! And more importantly, they are ghosts you know and love!

Everyone is watching and filming, so smile big!

A lady came into my office and told me that she'd been visiting her daughter. While they visited, they kept an eye on her granddaughter, sleeping on the couch in the living room. They were watching her through a nanny cam, and one of them noticed that the girl looked like she was falling off the couch, but was somehow hanging on. She was in a really strange suspended position, and they couldn't figure out how she didn't fall on her head. They went into the living room and, seeing that the little girl was awake, asked her, "You're almost on the floor—what are you doing?"

She told them, "Don't worry, she's holding me."

"Who?" they asked.

"The lady with the red fingernails."

I honestly don't recall who she said this woman was, maybe a neighbor or the other grandmother. I recall she was someone who had loved holding the little girl when she was just a baby but had crossed some time before. Without today's technology, they never would have witnessed that, and the little girl may never have thought to mention this encounter with "the lady with the red fingernails."

Another client shared a story about her son who was three years old, maybe a bit younger. One day my client's mother was visiting, and the two of them were in the kitchen, chatting. Her son was in his room, and she had the nanny cam on to keep an eye on him, but they weren't really paying close attention. At one point, her mother glanced over at the monitor and saw the child laughing and talking, waving his arms around. The two of them walked down the hall to his bedroom to see what had gotten him so excited. When they opened the door to the room, the boy turned around, pointed toward what appeared to be an empty wall in front of him, and said, "Pop!" The child had never known his grandfather, and he was the first grandchild, so he had never been taught the name "Pop-Pop." He then said, "Pop Don," which, taking into account that he hadn't yet mastered the letter *J*, they both realized must be "Poppa John," his grandfather's name. Although they were themselves convinced, they wanted my professional opinion as to whether the boy was actually talking with his deceased grandfather he had never met (at least not here on earth). Of course I agreed. I'm very certain that the two souls knew each other before the boy came back here. The grandfather may even have played a role in directing this soul to his current family. At a later date, my client was visiting her sister-in-law with her young son. The baby spied a photo of the grandfather, pointed to it, and said very clearly, "Pop Don." Everyone was speechless.

In addition to these, I've heard other stories of nanny cams and baby monitors letting parents in on a side of their young children's lives that used to be more inaccessible.

I've heard about new home technology—not only vacuum cleaners that whoosh across the carpet by themselves, but also refrigerators that notice what you are running low on and order it for you. I can hardly wait to see the fun the dead will have with that! Can you imagine? Pretty soon you'll have to inspect your grocery list to see if your deceased Uncle Sammy is ordering his favorite foods, just to let you know he's still hanging out in your kitchen.

Conclusion

At least ten years ago, a very nice gentleman, "Roy," came to one of my shows after learning about me through one of my books. His mother had passed away, and he was feeling completely bereft. He was in an "I'll try anything" place with his grief. I no longer remember what messages I was able to bring him from his mom, but whatever she told him, it brought him a lot of comfort.

Roy never forgot his experience, and he stayed in touch with me ever after. He told me he'd been a skeptic the first time he came to a show and had a reading, but he left converted. From then on, it was like I had a publicist in Pennsylvania; he was constantly telling everyone how much peace he'd found and insisting that they come to see me. I know this because there have been many guests at my shows over the years who have made a point of saying, "Roy sent me."

Roy was not just a publicist for me. He was an angel on earth. He would send me birthday cards and occasionally letters, always beginning with, "My Dear, Beautiful, Beloved Concetta," and ending with, "I hope I still make you smile." I never had the impression that he had a lot of money, but from time to time he would send me little gifts. Once he sent me a small jewelry box that was made in Israel because he'd heard me mention how connected I feel to the Jewish people. Once he sent me flowers. Usually when he called the office, he would end up talking with my assistant Elena, and they became close friends as well. When Elena called to let him know the flowers had been received and that he'd be hearing from me soon, he confided in her that he had never sent anyone flowers before.

What else can I say about Roy? He didn't drive, so he would only come to my shows when a friend could bring him. He wasn't very tall, he was gay, he never married, and he was very funny. Roy was an absolute dear, a pure soul, without a mean bone in his body. In short, both Elena and I loved him fiercely.

Roy passed away very recently. He'd been in hospice after battling throat cancer a second time. He felt defeated and didn't want to try any more. I had spoken with Roy by phone, and he told me that he wanted to be with his mom. He also asked me if I thought he might meet my brother Harold on the other side. Before we found out that Roy had crossed, Elena and I planned to visit him in hospice. He'd been such a good friend to us both, and we wanted to say goodbye in person. I can be very impulsive, but Elena wisely suggested that this should not be a surprise visit, that we should call to let Roy know we were coming. We set a day when we could clear our calendar, but when Elena called she was told by the staff that Roy had passed away the week before (see, psychics don't know everything). Oh my God, we were so upset, even though we both knew that Roy had wanted to go and was certainly at home and at peace.

We were meeting a few girlfriends at a local restaurant that evening, and, all the way there, we kept reminiscing about Roy. Then Elena turned to me and said, "Concetta, on my life, you will never get it out of me, but last time I was talking with Roy he gave me a word. He told me that if you ever said this word I should know that it was him saying 'I love you' to both of us."

Wow. Of course that made me totally crazy. My first impulse was to say, "What was the word?" This went nowhere, as Elena immediately reminded me that she'd been sworn to secrecy and would never tell. But as we pulled up to the restaurant, I got a sudden jolt.

"Elena!" I said. "Roy's here."

"He is?" she asked.

"Yes! And he's trying to tell me the word."

"O-kaay," she said. "What is he saying?"

I said, "He's trying to show me...it's got something to do with food."

"Yeeah?" said Elena.

"Yeah. I'm not saying it's ice cream, but it's something you can eat with ice cream."

Elena says, "Ye-e-ess."

I said, "But it's also something you could have for breakfast."

Elena says, "Ye-e-ess."

I said, "It's either *waffle* or *crepe*!"

Elena goes, "Oh my God! The word was *waffle*! Roy told me his favorite thing in the world was Belgian waffles!"

I think the two of us were not sure whether to laugh out loud or cry. Anyway, *nailed it!* I could not wait to go in and brag to our girlfriends waiting for us in the restaurant.

There's a little more to the waffle story. The day Elena and I had planned to visit Roy, of course, we now had nowhere else to go. So Elena said, "Look, we never have a free day, but we cleared the calendar today. You've never seen my new house, so why don't I pick you up? I'll show you my house, we'll have lunch and just spend a relaxing day together."

Elena lives in an area that has a lot of really cute restaurants, so when she said she'd cook, I told her I didn't want to put her to any trouble, but she insisted. She likes to cook, and she'd already bought everything, saying, "I can make either chicken or pasta, whichever you prefer." I told her I felt in need of comfort food, so pasta it was. Elena went to her cupboard and pulled down a box the size of a large shoebox, filled with probably hundreds of recipes. She told me, "I've made this lots of times, but if I don't follow the recipe closely I always screw up the sauce." When she opened the lid of the box, lying right on top was a recipe for... Belgian waffles. Both our mouths were hanging open. Under that recipe was a photo of Elena's husband and son—a photo she always keeps *on top* so it's the first thing she sees when she opens the box. She said to me, "I can't even remember the last time I made Belgian waffles!"

Did it stop there? No. Elena's son came home from college, and she told him the whole story. He said, "That's crazy. I eat at the cafeteria all the time. Our breakfasts are always the same—eggs, pancakes, bacon, ham, toast, fruit...and that's pretty much it. Last week I went in and there was a sign at the front that said, 'Special Today: Belgian Waffles.' "

That's gotta be the end, right? Nope. The following Sunday, I went out with the girls to a little diner we've been to many times. We had our meals and a nice chat, and then the waitress comes to ask if anyone wants dessert. Before any of us can order, she says, "Just to let you know, we have a special today: Belgian waffles."

Yes, Roy, you are still making me smile.

I found myself thinking a lot about Roy, as we all do when someone we care about passes. I remembered him asking me if I thought he would get to meet Harold once he was in heaven. I imagine one day I may be talking with Harold and he'll tell me that he's got a new friend there who just loves Belgian waffles. I'll keep you posted on that. But this made me think about Harold, and how alike in some ways he and Roy are. Both have a great sense of humor—Harold was one of the funniest guys I've ever known—but more importantly, both of them were incredibly kind when they were on this side of the veil.

Another time, Elena called me when I was driving to say that I'd received a call from a woman named Christine who said she knew my brother. She had, by happenstance, been reading my book *Do Dead People Watch You Shower?*, in which I talk about Harold, and she realized that the person I was writing about was someone she had lived with some decades ago. Elena gave me her number, and I called her right away. The story she told me blew me away, and yet it was unsurprising. It was the 1970s, and she had come through a hard divorce with no one to help her get back on her feet, and she had nowhere to live. The two were introduced by a mutual friend, and Harold told her that he had a two-bedroom apartment and that she was welcome to stay with him. He hardly knew her, but he helped her through a really difficult time. She told me a number of really beautiful things he had done while they lived together, and I was in tears as I drove, listening on my Bluetooth. Hanging up, after our conversation, I spoke to God, saying, "Please bless my beautiful brother Harold." I said a long prayer, actually, and as I was finishing it, I heard Harold himself say that a surprise was coming my way. When I arrived home and walked in my door, the phone was ringing. It was my agent letting me know that we had an offer for my new book—the book you are now reading. This was a very nice surprise, and one that I feel Harold had a hand in, since he has been involved in my public career right from the get-go.

Here's one more story about Harold. There was a blizzard in New York during the 1970s—I can't recall the exact year. Harold was a smoker and decided to brave the cold to walk to a bodega for cigarettes. He wore only a short black leather jacket over his usual get-up of T-shirt and jeans. On his way to the store, he was mugged by some young thugs. He offered his money, but they demanded his jacket too. Then they beat him unconscious. The snow kept coming down until he was completely covered by it. He was discovered the next day with a broken arm and other injuries. When I first saw him, I was going nuts about these scum who had attacked him. He told me that, when he woke up in the hospital, there was a crucifix hanging on the wall. He found himself staring at it, contemplating it. He thought, "Yes, He forgave those who hurt Him. So I will forgive these men." My mouth was just hanging open. But he really meant it.

In the short time he was here, my brother gave me many lessons that are taking me an entire lifetime to absorb. Generosity. Forgiveness. Simple kindness. These are the things that I hear also, constantly, from the other side. There, we know perfect peace, but peace on earth is our true goal, to become closer to God and to make earth more like heaven. This is our reality show, and we're writing it as we go along. We have free will here.

We need to think on our feet and can make the experience a comedy or a tragedy, depending on how we choose to act.

We face enormous challenges here on the physical plane, but the spirits of those we've loved and who love us are Always In Reach and will try to help. You can ask these folks for anything. If you just reach out to them sincerely, they will comfort you, they will see the goodness in you, and they will put their arms around you. Don't be afraid. Tell them what you want, your desires. Remember that God said, "Whatever you ask the Father in my name, he may give it to you." God wants each of us to have our heart's desire, so long as no one else is harmed. God is good, and all of us, whether in flesh or in spirit, are pieces of God.

I love you all.

Concetta

A Little Extra Sauce

Being Italian, I never turn down a serving of good pasta if I can help it, and so much the better if there's extra! There were a few fun stories I wanted to fit in here, but they didn't seem to go in any particular place. Then I realized they did have a common thread...

At one of my big shows, I called on a woman in the audience who was sitting with her two daughters. The woman's mother had died somewhat recently, and they were hoping to hear from her. The woman had a great sense of humor. As her mother was saying all these things that were getting big smiles from the three of them, she confirmed, "That would be my mother. She was always trying to make us laugh!" Her mother also said that the woman had taken a lot of things home from her house and she was happy that she'd taken things that her mother had loved and now she would have them to love. She mentioned a number of little tiny things, including a little tchotchke in her kitchen—a little pink figurine of a girl holding a baby. Her mother had always told her that it reminded her of when her daughter was born. The woman confirmed that she recognized the items her mother had described.

Then her mother said, "Tell her I know, that I heard what she said about the refrigerator." I had no idea what that meant, but the woman and her daughters cracked up. She told me, "We were all saying, 'What are we going to do now, without Grandma's sauce?'" She meant her spaghetti sauce, or "red gravy" as we call it in New Jersey. She said, "We were all saying, 'What are we gonna do? Nobody ever made it like Grandma!'"

But then, happily enough, in her mother's refrigerator freezer compartment she'd found a container of her mother's red gravy.

As I mentioned, the three of them loved hearing from their mother and grandmother, laughing along with the fun memories. But when it came to the sauce, they all started to cry—no doubt thinking about how much they were going to miss this funny lady and the great gravy she used to make.

At another show, I was reading for a woman whose mother had passed away. During the reading I said, "You have something in your kitchen that your mother is asking me to mention. It's not dishes—it seems like some kind of appliance, something you *do* something with." I told her that her mother was saying something about this thing being "back." The woman laughed and told me this story...

When her mother passed, her father decided to downsize and move to Florida to live near one of his other children. He wanted to have a big garage sale to get rid of extra stuff. This woman, the daughter who lived near him, helped him with the sale, but wasn't paying a lot of attention to what he put up for sale. So it wasn't until afterward that she realized that among the sold items was—are you ready for this?—a spaghetti strainer. Apparently this strainer was her grandmother's before it was her mother's. It was, if you will, an "heirloom spaghetti strainer," so it actually held meaning for her. She was really upset. She didn't know who had bought it; it was just gone. Of course, this is one of life's small tragedies that we just have to take a deep breath and let go of, but it still stung.

Some little while later, the woman was invited to the home of a friend of a friend for some kind of gathering. In the course of

the evening, she was in the hostess's kitchen and her eye fell
on a spaghetti strainer. She said, "Oh my God, that looks like
my mother's strainer!" The strainer had a particular dent in the
pedestal. She was familiar with it—she'd handled it many, many
times. She said she actually started to cry. She said to the hostess,
"Where did you get this strainer?" And the woman told her she
had bought it at a garage sale.

The hostess was so taken by her grief, she said, "By all means,
you must take the strainer. It means nothing to me." And she was
happy to give the woman this object that meant so much to her.

Obviously, it's not just us Italians who feel strongly about our
food. I was chatting with a client before we got into her reading
and she told me that her mother's sisters all cooked, but now her
aunts had all passed, and she had no recipes from anybody. The
one thing she desperately wanted was a recipe for pierogies—
those delicious filled dumplings from Poland. Her family had had
a particular recipe that she'd always loved, but with her mother
and aunts all gone, she had no way of finding out how they
made them.

During the reading, I told her that she was going to get
something from Florida. She didn't have any idea what it could
be, so she just let it go and didn't think much about it.

Not four months later, I got a call from her, and she was all
excited. She had gone to visit a relative in Florida, who told her,
"You have some other relatives here, who knew your mother, but
whom you've never met, and they want to meet you."

She was thrilled and said, "Oh, I'd love to meet them."

When they met, the relative said to her, "You know, years ago, your mother gave me a recipe for pierogies that I still make to this day."

She said, "What? Can you give me the recipe?" She got the recipe and it came from Florida, just as we'd learned during the reading. She said, "Concetta, to me, getting that recipe was like getting a million dollars."

Acknowledgments

Stephany Evans, my dear friend and literary agent. I could not have done this book or many other things without YOU! Your talent and dedication are whole-heartedly appreciated. Thank you, my dear friend, I truly love you with all my heart.

Ginger Grancagnolo. You have single-handedly brought me back to my faith, for which I will eternally thank you! You have enriched my life in so many ways; you are a teacher in immeasurable ways! I love you, dearest Tink!

Elena Oswald. My sweet Elena Baby! It seems we have been at this for a very long time! Your contribution to my work and my life is teaching me that family never leaves you! I am so grateful you have hung in there with me! From the day I met you, I knew we would be together forever! I love you, my darling girl!

Leanna Russo. Thank you Lee-lee for taking the job! Thank you for finding solutions we so desperately needed! You have come to mean very much to me! I wish you all the happiness in the world always!

Jessica Bertoldi. We sure have come a long way! You're the daughter from another mother I always wanted! Thank you for always being available to travel with me, to talk with, to laugh and cry! Your confidence in me has always brought me comfort and joy! I love you, daughter, forever!

Debra Malanga. You're the girlfriend everyone wants! A loyal and trusted friend! Thank you for your input in this book and for always being such a beautiful friend to me! I love you, girlfriend!

Cornelia DiNunzio. A.k.a. Mushy! While you now reside in Florida, I still can count on you for help in so many ways, and you never let me down! I love you, baby!

Madeline Krawse. Every time I need a print-out or help, you come to the rescue. I thank you so much! I love you! ♥

Debra Casha. Thank you for being so supportive to me, in my work and in my life. I love you!

Joanne Candito. Thank you for always listening to and caring for me! You're a great friend, and I love you! ♥

Antonio Barone. Thank you for so much! Doing the driveway when it is snow-covered, going way out of your way for both John and me: thank you for so many things. You have showed John and me so much love. We love you like a son! ♥

Leticia Peralta. My Darling friend, I will never forget the first time I met you. I knew we would be friends forever. You say I saved you, and I say we saved each other. Thank you for opening your beautiful home to me! I love you forever.

Ila Blumrosen. My friend and manager. I adore you and will forever thank you for believing in me and taking me to my beloved Mexico. I love you!

Talina Fernandez. My dear friend. You have always been very kind and generous to me. Thank you from the bottom of my heart. I love you!

My beloved Mendez family—Barbara, Louis, and family. I will forever carry you all in my heart. All of your generous acts of love will Never Be Forgotten. I love each and every one of you!

The PPPs. You know who you are! My life is so LOVE-filled because of our times spent together! I cannot say enough how much I love each and every one of you.

MY DEAR CLIENTS! I could talk forever about you—my heart is so filled with love for the many people I have met along my way of work. For the great difference you have all made in my life and the amazing love I have been shown by so many folks, I thank you all so very much!!!! I truly love and appreciate you all!

My family and friends. I would like to mention by name each and every one of you, however that would be twenty pages, so let me say this: life would be empty without you all! I feel extremely lucky to have the people in my life that I have! I pray God allows me to continue doing what I do, with all of you by my side. I love you deeply forever.

And last, but never least, thank you to Brenda Knight, my Mango editor, for believing in my new book. And thank you to Chris McKenney and ALL the Mango team for making this baby a reality!

About the Author

Psychic medium and New York Times bestselling author Concetta Bertoldi has been able to see the other side since childhood. Her first book Do Dead People Watch You Shower? And Other Questions You've Been All But Dying to Ask a Medium hit the New York Times bestseller list in 2008. She followed that success with a sequel Do Dead People Walk Their Dogs? Questions You'd Ask a Medium if You Had the Chance and Inside the Other Side: Soul Contracts, Life Lessons and How Dead People Help Us Between Here and Heaven. Her books have sold over 150,000 copies. She has a very long waiting list for private readings, and her clients range from members of Britain's royal family to Hollywood celebrities, politicians, and everyone in between.

Featured in such media as Time magazine and on The Early Show on CBS, she travels throughout the United States and Mexico doing live events that include psychic readings for standing-room-only crowds.

She lives in New Jersey with her skeptical husband John.